Oxford Discover
Workbook 2

Lesley Koustaff   **Susan Rivers**

1 How are animals different from one another?
- Unit 1 2
- Unit 2 10

2 How do things change?
- Unit 3 20
- Unit 4 28

3 How are things different now from long ago?
- Unit 5 38
- Unit 6 46

4 When do we use subtraction?
- Unit 7 56
- Unit 8 64

5 How do people get along with each other?
- Unit 9 74
- Unit 10 82

6 Why should we take care of the Earth?
- Unit 11 92
- Unit 12 100

7 How does music make us feel?
- Unit 13 110
- Unit 14 118

8 What makes things move?
- Unit 15 128
- Unit 16 136

9 How do we make art?
- Unit 17 146
- Unit 18 154

Student's Writing Resource 164

OXFORD
UNIVERSITY PRESS

SBC
PROPERTY OF
SUMMER BOARDING COURSES LTD

BIG QUESTION 1

How are animals different from one another?

Think about the Big Question. Write.

What do you know?

_____
_____
_____
_____
_____
_____
_____

What do you want to know?

_____
_____
_____
_____
_____
_____
_____

UNIT 1 — Get Ready

Words

A Circle two words for each picture.

1. (scales) / (gills) / feathers

2. eggs / mammal / wings

3. gills / skin / feathers

4. mammal / scales / fur

5. amphibians / wings / skin

Vocabulary: Animals and Animal Body Parts

B Write the correct words.

1. gills
2. _____ 
3. _____ 
4. _____ 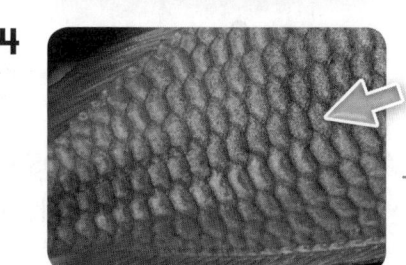
5. _____ 
6. _____

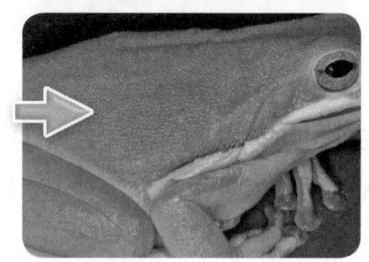

C Circle the odd one out.

1. (feathers)   gills   scales
2. gills   fur   amphibian
3. wings   scales   feathers
4. eggs   mammal   fur

D Complete the chart.

wings   fur   gills   feathers   ~~scales~~

Fish	Mammal	Bird
1 scales	3 _____	4 _____
2 _____		5 _____

Vocabulary: Animals and Animal Body Parts **Unit 1**   3

Read

A Read the text quickly. Answer the questions.
Where do lions live? Where do whales live?

Lions and Whales

In some ways lions and whales are the same, and in some ways they're different.

Lions live on land. They have fur on their bodies to keep them warm. They have four legs and can run fast. Whales live in the ocean. They have skin on their bodies. They don't have legs. They have fins to help them swim.

Think
How are lions different from whales?

Lions and whales are both mammals. They have tails and big teeth. They catch and eat other animals. Their babies are born alive, and they drink milk from their mothers.

Think
How are lions the same as whales?

4   **Unit 1**   *Reading: Compare and Contrast*   Student Book page 9

Understand

Comprehension

A What part of the text do you like? Check (✓).

The lions ☐   The whales ☐   Their babies ☐

B Read the text again. What is the same? What is different? Check (✓) the correct column.

	Same	Different
1 Where they live		✓
2 What covers their bodies		
3 What they eat		
4 How they move		
5 The animal group		
6 The number of legs they have		
7 What their babies drink		

C Circle *True* or *False*.

1. Lions live in the ocean.   True   **(False)**
2. Fur keeps a lion cool.   True   False
3. Lions can walk and run.   True   False
4. Whales can run.   True   False
5. Whales have small teeth.   True   False
6. Whales can swim.   True   False
7. Lions and whales are amphibians.   True   False
8. Lions and whales eat other animals.   True   False
9. Lion and whale babies are born alive.   True   False
10. Lion and whale babies stay with their mothers.   True   False

Grammar in Use

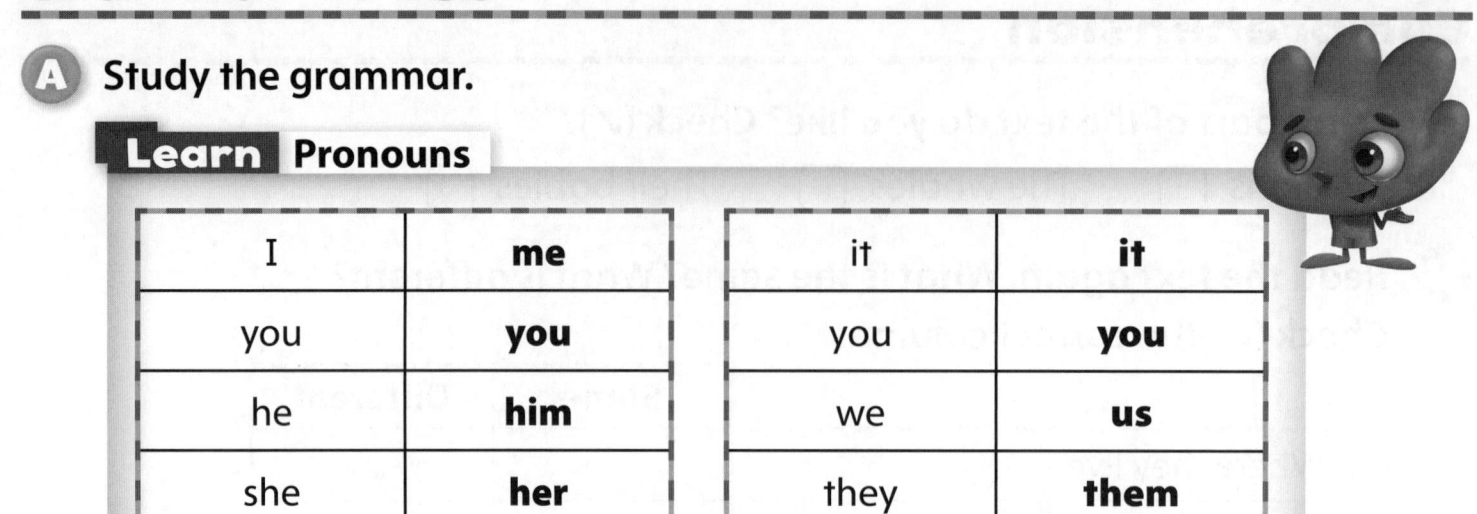

A Study the grammar.

Learn Pronouns

I	**me**
you	**you**
he	**him**
she	**her**

it	**it**
you	**you**
we	**us**
they	**them**

B Match the beginnings to the ends of the sentences.

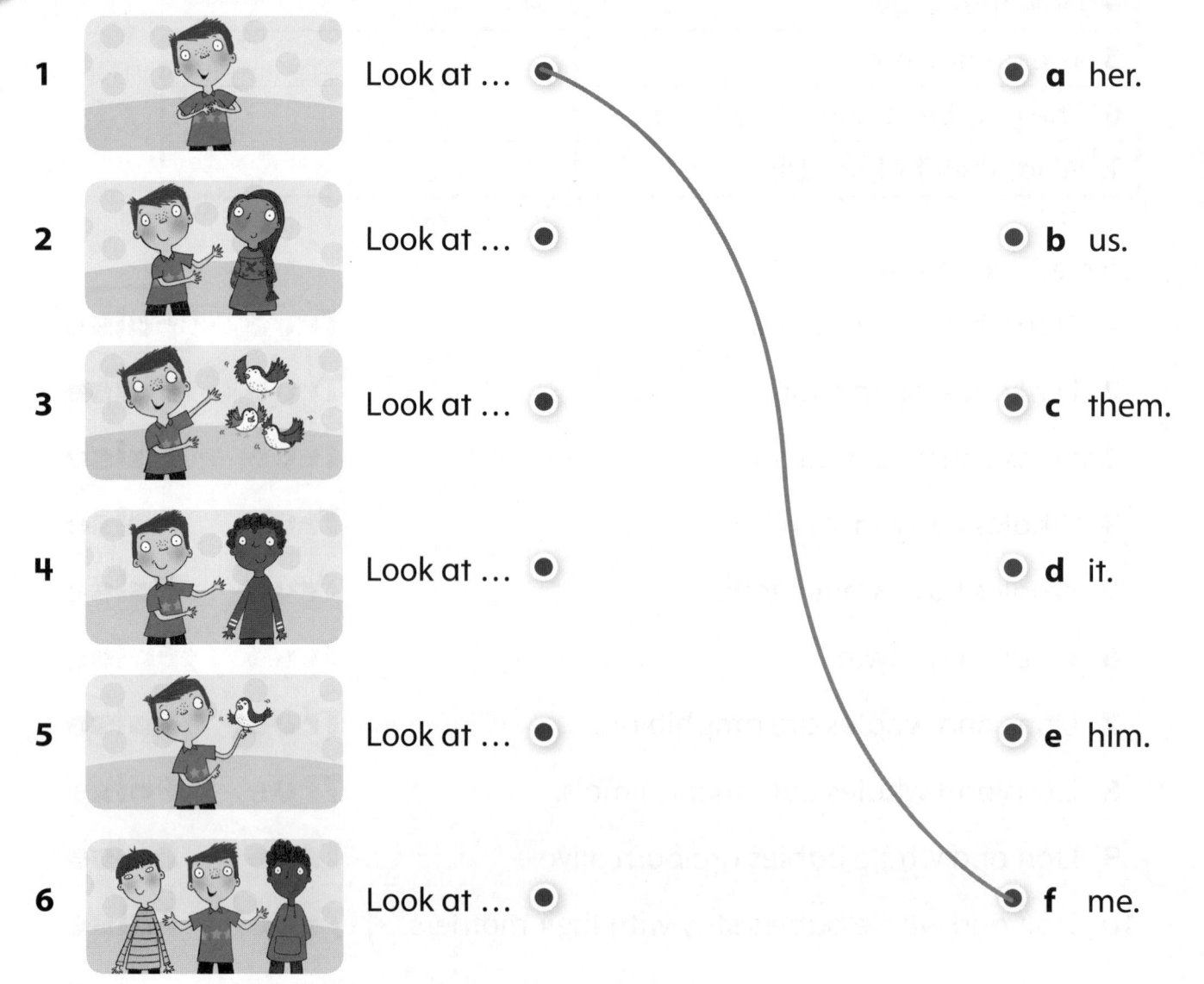

1. Look at … **a** her.
2. Look at … **b** us.
3. Look at … **c** them.
4. Look at … **d** it.
5. Look at … **e** him.
6. Look at … **f** me.

6   Unit 1   *Grammar: Subject and Object Pronouns*   Student Book page 13

C Match the people and animals to the pronouns.

1 my brother
2 the lion
3 my cousin and I
4 the cat and the dog
5 Ana

a she
b they
c he
d we
e it

f him
g us
h it
i them
j her

D Circle the correct words.

1 Birds have wings. Wings help **us** / **(them)** fly.
2 My father is playing the drums. Listen to **him** / **her**.
3 The goldfish has gills. They help **them** / **it** breathe.
4 I am dancing. Look at **you** / **me**.
5 We can't bake a pie. Please teach **us** / **you**.
6 We're friends. You like me, and I like **me** / **you**.

E Circle the words and write.

1 Do you know Leonardo DiCaprio?
   Yes / (No), I **know** / **(don't know)** _____him_____ .

2 Do you help your mother?
   Yes / No, I **help** / **don't help** _____ .

3 Do you like cats?
   Yes / No, I **like** / **don't like** _____ .

4 Do you like math?
   Yes / No, I **like** / **don't like** _____ .

5 Does Leonardo DiCaprio know you and your friend?
   Yes / No, he **knows** / **doesn't know** _____ .

Grammar: Subject and Object Pronouns   Unit 1   7

Communicate

Words

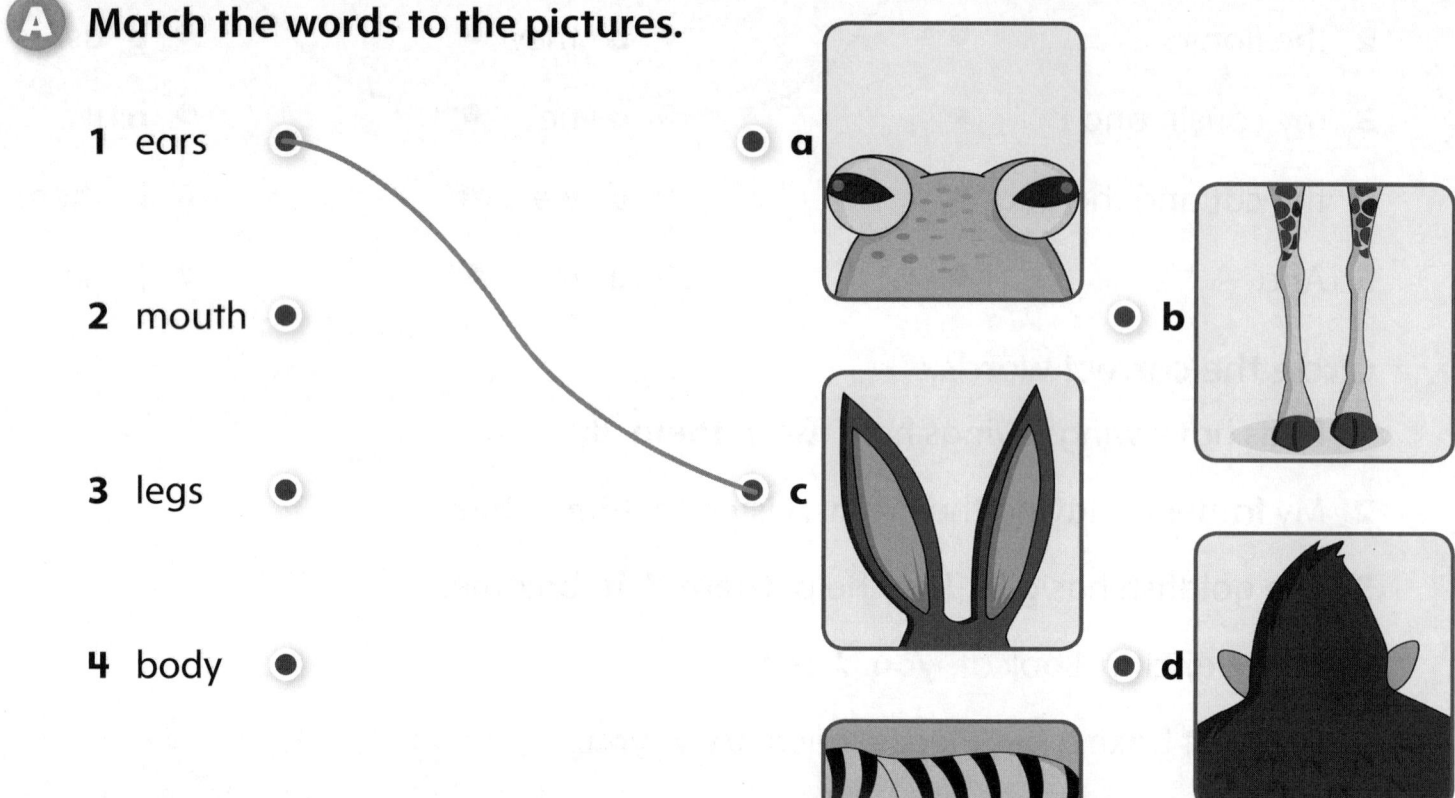

A Match the words to the pictures.

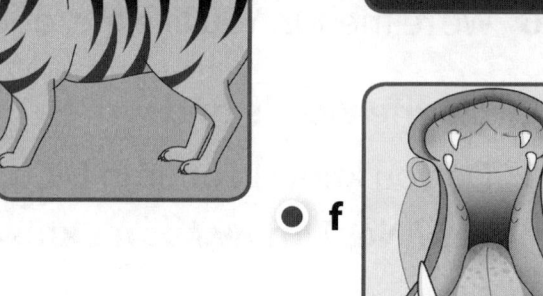

1 ears
2 mouth
3 legs
4 body
5 eyes
6 head

a
b
c
d
e
f

B Complete the sentences.

1 I have one _____mouth_____. I use it to talk, eat, and drink.
2 I have two _____. They help me run fast.
3 I see with my _____. I can open and close them.
4 I listen to music with my _____. I have two.
5 In the sunshine I wear a hat on my _____.
6 In winter I wear a coat to keep my _____ warm.

8   Unit 1   *Vocabulary: Body Parts*   Student Book page 14

Word Study

A Circle the compound word and write it.

1 The (starfish) doesn't have scales. _____starfish_____

2 My backpack is red and blue. _____

3 The orangutan lives in a rainforest. _____

4 A bluebird has feathers to keep it warm. _____

5 Look at the butterfly on that flower. _____

6 Look at that big, yellow sunflower! _____

Writing

A Read about Mark's favorite animal group.

> Fish is my favorite animal group. They live in water. They have gills to help them breathe. They have fins and tails to help them swim. They lay eggs in the water.

B Answer the questions.

What's your favorite animal group? _____

Where do they live? _____

What things do they have? _____

What do they do? _____

C Now write about your favorite animal group.

_____

_____

_____

_____

_____

UNIT 2 Get Ready

Words

A Look at the pictures and circle the correct word.

1. (peck) / escape
2. fish / worm
3. squawk / pinecone
4. berries / peck
5. escape / fight
6. hunt / fight

B Complete the chart.

creep   berries   fight   ~~worm~~   squawk

Things Animals Eat
1. worm
2. _____

Things Animals Do
3. _____
4. _____
5. _____

10   Unit 2   *Vocabulary: Animal Words and Verbs*   Student Book page 16

C What's next? Read and match.

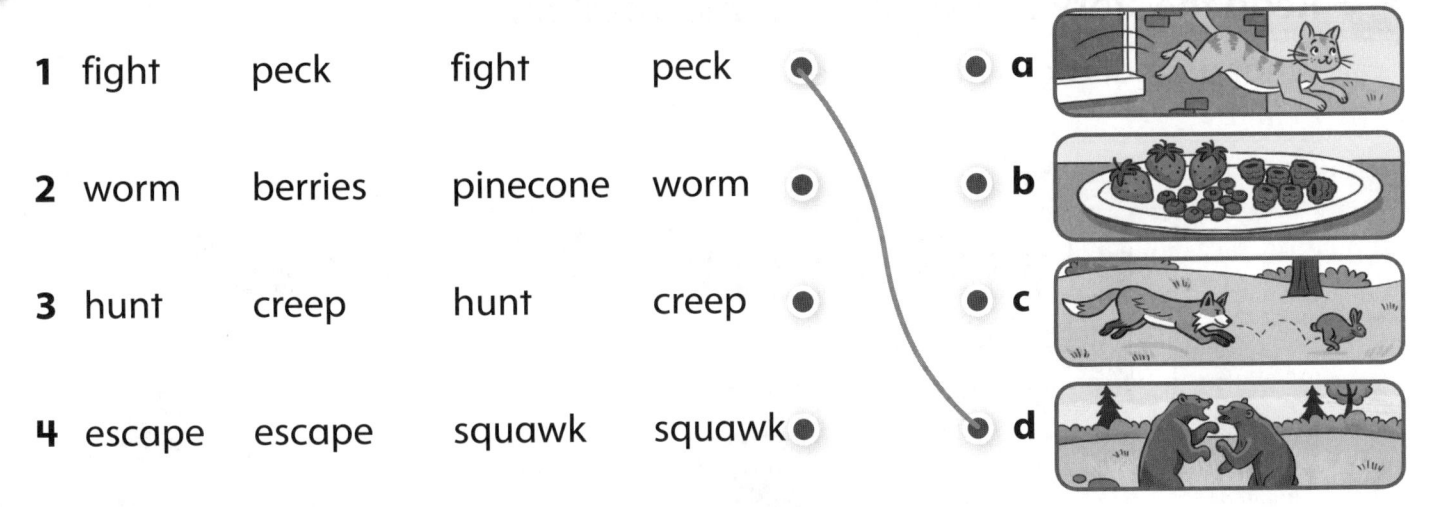

1 fight   peck   fight   peck   • a
2 worm   berries pinecone worm   • b
3 hunt   creep   hunt   creep   • c
4 escape   escape   squawk   squawk •   • d

D Read the clues. Complete the crossword.

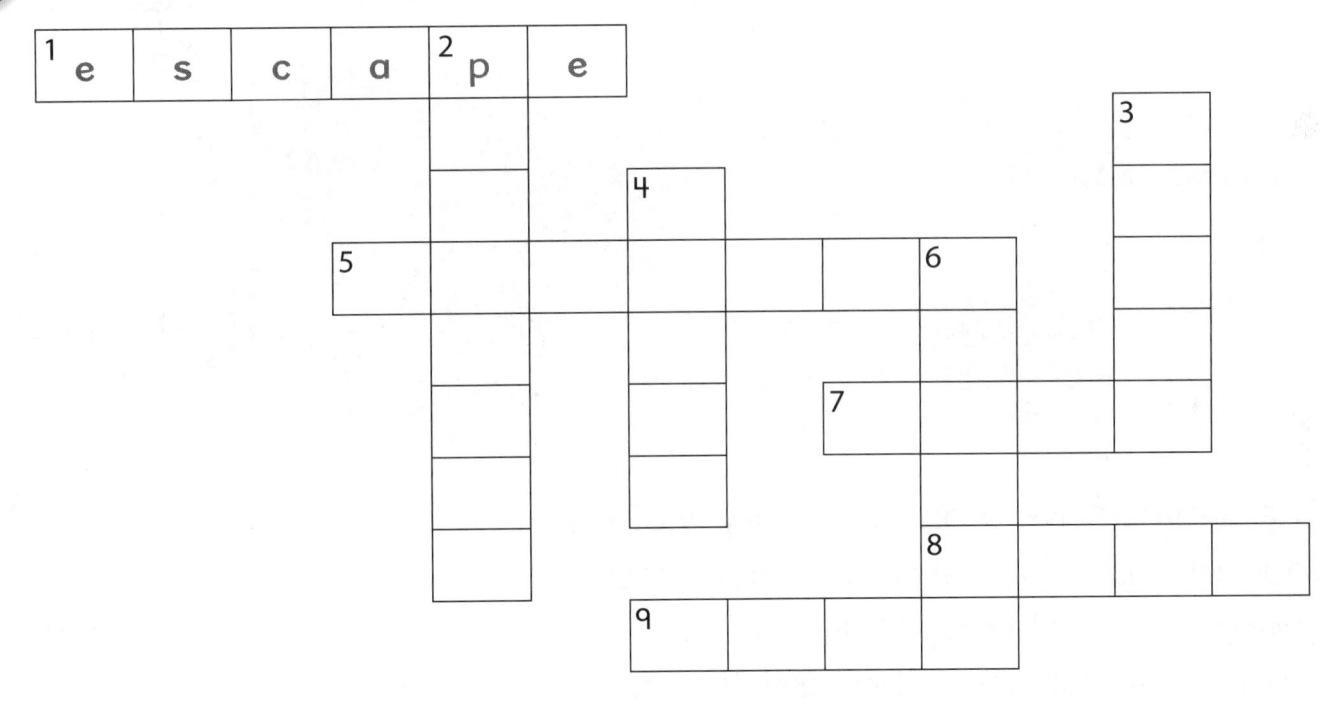

| 1 e | s | c | a | 2 p | e |

Across →
1 To get away from a place.
5 Small, red fruits.
7 Animals do this to catch food.
8 A long thin animal without legs.
9 Birds do this with their food.

Down ↓
2 It grows on pine trees.
3 Brothers and sisters sometimes do this.
4 Cats can do this very quietly.
6 Birds can make this funny sound loudly.

Vocabulary: Animal Words and Verbs **Unit 2**

Read

A **Read the story quickly. Answer the question.**
What animals does the cat see?

Unusual Friends

The Smiths have a big cat, Molly. Molly is loud and playful, but always friendly and gentle. One cold day Molly sees two small, quiet rabbits in the yard. They're cold and alone.

Molly carries the rabbits to the door and meows. They're scared. The Smiths come out. They make a big and warm cage for the rabbits to sleep in. The rabbits are happy. They're gentle, and Molly likes them.

Sometimes they play with Molly in the yard, and they never fight.

Think
How is Molly different from the rabbits?

Think
How is Molly the same as the rabbits?

Unit 2 Reading: Compare and Contrast

Student Book page 17

Understand

Comprehension

A What part of the story do you like? Check (✓).

Molly ☐   The rabbits ☐   The Smiths ☐

B Compare and contrast Molly and the rabbits. Write the words in the Venn diagram.

~~loud~~   gentle   small   quiet   big

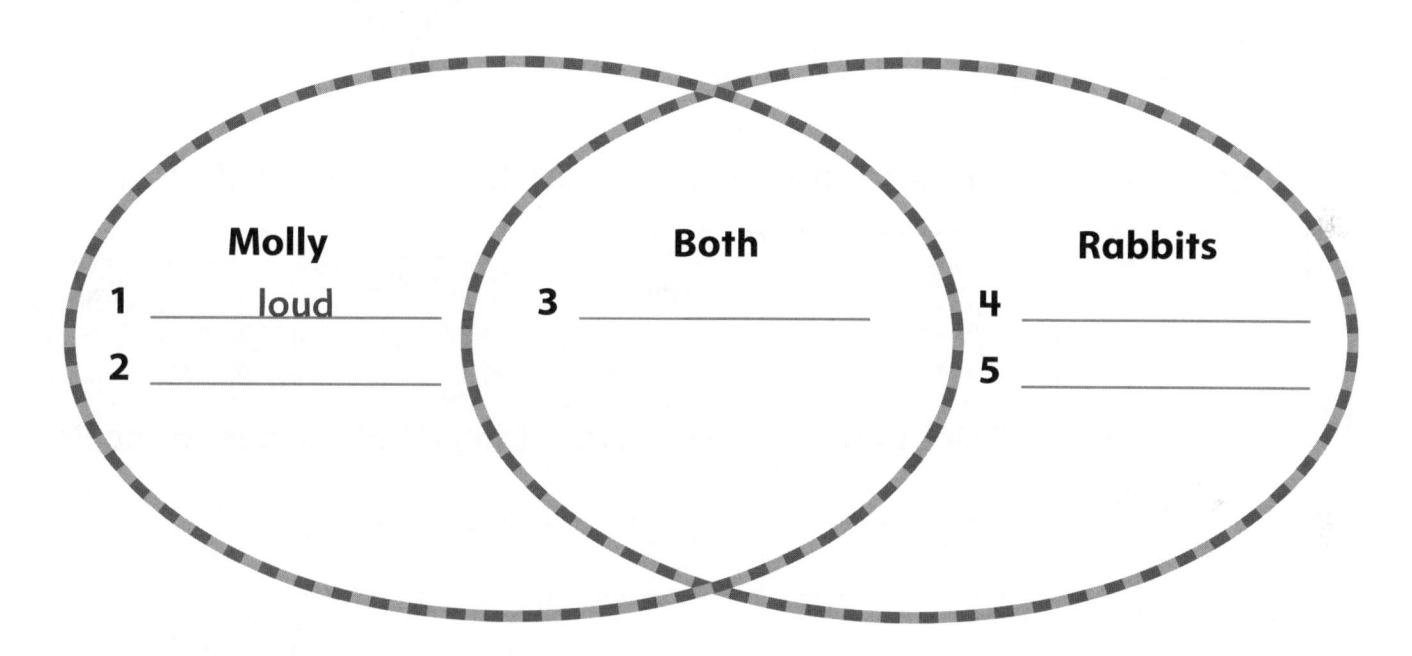

Molly
1 ____loud____
2 _____

Both
3 _____

Rabbits
4 _____
5 _____

C Circle *True* or *False*.

1 Molly is a friendly bird.   True   **(False)**
2 It is a cold day when Molly finds the rabbits.   True   False
3 The rabbits sleep with Molly in the kennel.   True   False
4 The rabbits are lonely at the Smith's house.   True   False
5 Molly and the rabbits are friends at the end of the story.   True   False
6 The Smiths are nice people.   True   False

Comprehension   Unit 2   13

Grammar in Use

A Study the grammar.

Learn Frequency

I you we they	always usually sometimes hardly ever never	fight.
he she it		fights.

B Look at the chart and read the sentences. Write *T* (True) or *F* (False).

	Drinks Milk	Eats Fish	Plays Ball	Goes To the Park
Jim	✓✓✓	✓✓	✓✓✓	✓
Amy	✓✓	✗	✓	✓✓
Roy	✗	✗	✓✓✓	✓✓
Rosie	✓✓	✓✓✓	✗	✓

always	usually	sometimes	hardly ever	never
✓✓✓✓	✓✓✓	✓✓	✓	✗

1 Jim sometimes drinks milk. __F__

2 Amy never goes to the park. ____

3 Roy never eats fish. ____

4 Rosie usually plays ball. ____

C Look at the chart again. Circle the correct words.
1. Rosie **usually / (sometimes)** drinks milk.
2. Amy **always / never** eats fish.
3. Roy **sometimes / hardly ever** goes to the park.
4. Jim **always / usually** plays ball.
5. Rosie **never / hardly ever** goes to the park.
6. Amy **usually / always** drinks milk.

D Now complete the sentences.
1. Jim ____hardly ever____ goes to the park.
2. Roy _____ drinks milk.
3. Amy _____ plays ball.
4. Rosie _____ eats fish.
5. Amy and Roy _____ eat fish.
6. Jim _____ eats fish.
7. Roy _____ plays ball.
8. Jim _____ drinks milk.
9. Amy _____ goes to the park.
10. Rosie _____ plays ball.

E Complete the sentences.
1. I _____ drink milk.
2. I _____ eat fish.
3. I _____ play ball.
4. I _____ go to the park.
5. I _____ play in the yard.
6. I _____ fight with my friends.
7. I _____ clean my room.
8. I _____ help my mum.

Grammar: Adverbs of Frequency Unit 2 **15**

Communicate

Words

A Look at the words. Write the numbers.

1 calm   3 gentle   5 strong
2 fierce   4 patient   6 smart

a ___   b ___   c ___
d ___   e 1   f ___

B Look at the picture. Complete the sentences.

| calm   fierce   gentle   strong |

1 The goldfish is _____.
2 The man is _____.
3 The cat is _____.
4 The snake is _____.

16 Unit 2 *Vocabulary: Adjectives*   Student Book page 22

Writing Study

A Match the sentences to the pronouns. Then rewrite the sentences.

1. Fur keeps <u>the squirrels</u> warm.
2. <u>My mother</u> is giving me a cookie.
3. You like <u>Clara and me</u>.
4. <u>Wings</u> help the honeybee fly.
5. <u>Your brother</u> is very strong.
6. We like <u>Emily</u>.

a he
b they
c her
d them   Fur keeps them warm.
e she
f us

Writing

A Read about Coco, the cat.

My friend has a cat. Its name is Coco. Coco is very calm. It never runs around. It's very smart, too. It watches TV! Coco isn't fierce. It never fights with other cats.

B Answer the questions about an animal you know.

What animal is it? _____
Does it have a name? _____
Is it smart / calm / noisy? _____
What does it always / never do? _____

C Now write about that animal.

What have you learned?

_____

Review

A Complete the puzzles. Find and write the secret words.

1

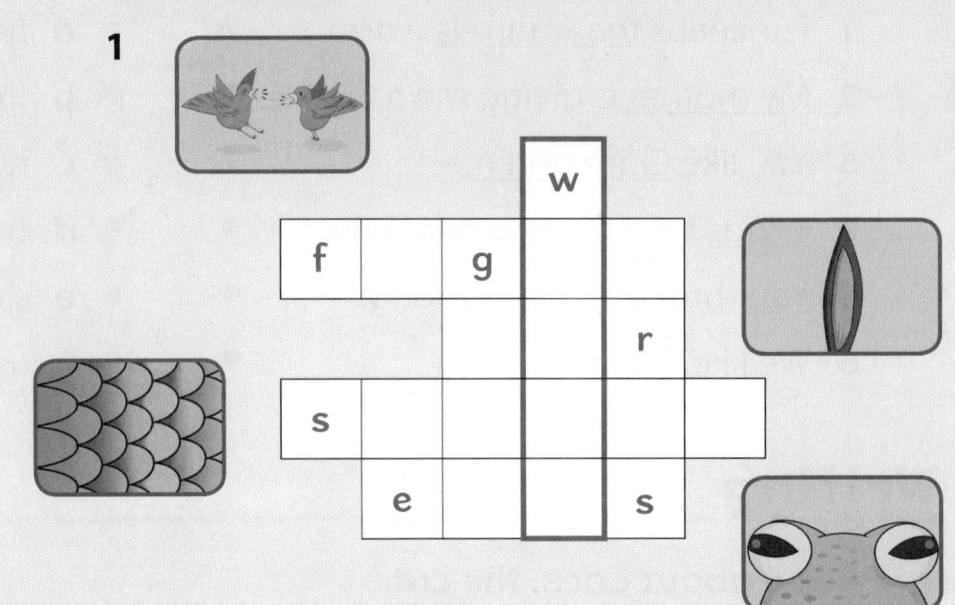

The secret word is _____.

2

The secret word is _____.

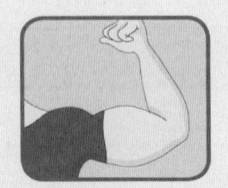

BIG QUESTION 1
How are animals different from one another?

18

B Find and circle six words.

yizgillspke(berries)crtaescapewqouiheadvxerwquietdrofightxolp

C Write the sentences in the correct order.
1. keeps / fur / warm / them / .
   Fur keeps them warm.
2. fight / and / Leo / never / Lily / .
3. with / plays / sometimes / ball / Billy / us / .
4. us / the teacher / books / gives / .
5. hardly ever / that / squawks / bird / .
6. him / you / like / .

D Circle the pronouns and underline the compound words.
1. (He) is buying a <u>goldfish</u> for (her).
2. They are building a snowman with us.
3. We are playing a game in her bedroom.
4. My mother is reading a storybook to me.
5. Give him the football.
6. Bea is baking gingerbread cookies for you.

Review 19

BIG QUESTION 2

How do things change?

Think about the Big Question. Write.

What do you know?

_____
_____
_____
_____
_____
_____
_____

What do you want to know?

_____
_____
_____
_____
_____
_____
_____

UNIT 3 — Get Ready

Words

A Check (✓) the correct picture.

1 flow

☐ a    ✓ b

2 gas

☐ a    ☐ b

3 freeze

☐ a    ☐ b

20   Unit 3   *Vocabulary: Forms and States*   Student Book page 28

B Look at the picture and write the words.

~~liquid~~   steam   melt   ice   heat   solid

1 _____
2 _____
3 _____
4 _____
5 __liquid__
6 _____

C Match the beginnings to the ends of the sentences.

1 A drum is — d a solid.
2 Soda is — a a liquid.
3 Air is — e a gas.
4 Water can — c melt.
5 Snow can — b freeze.

D Complete the sentences.

1 I make something hot. I ____heat____ it.
2 We make _____ by heating water.
3 Steam is a _____.
4 I _____ water. It is now ice.

Vocabulary: Forms and States   Unit 3   **21**

Read

A **Read the text quickly. Answer the question.**

What happens to water in hot springs?

Hot Springs

Hot springs are small lakes with hot water. In some hot springs, hot rocks on the ground of the spring heat the water. In others, the water heats up under the ground.

When the water is very hot, some of it changes to steam. The water was a liquid, and now it's steam, a gas.

When hot steam meets warm air, we can't see a lot of steam. When hot steam meets very cold air, we can see a lot of steam.

Be careful in hot springs! The hot water and hot steam can be dangerous.

Think

What's the cause of the hot water?
What's the effect of the hot water?

Understand

Comprehension

A What part of the text do you like? Check (✓).

The lakes ☐   The hot rocks ☐   The steam ☐

B Read the causes and effects. Circle *True* or *False*. Correct the false statements.

Causes	Effects
1 The water is very hot.	Some of it changes to steam. **(True)** False
2 Hot steam meets warm air.	We can see a lot of steam. **True** **False**
3 Hot steam meets very cold air.	We can't see a lot of steam. **True** **False**

C Answer the questions.

1 How does water in hot springs get hot? Name two ways.
   a <u>Hot rocks on the ground of the spring heat the water.</u>
   b _____

2 What is a solid at a hot spring?
   _____

3 What is a liquid at a hot spring?
   _____

4 What is a gas at a hot spring?
   _____

5 Why should you be careful at hot springs?
   _____

Comprehension Unit 3   23

Grammar in Use

A Study the grammar.

Learn Simple Past of Verb *To Be*

Now		
I	am / am not	hot.
he / she / it	is / isn't	
you / we / they	are / aren't	

Then		
I / he / she / it	was / wasn't	hot.
you / we / they	were / weren't	

B Circle the correct words.

1 The water **was** / **were** very hot.

2 The feathers **was** / **were** soft.

3 The boy **wasn't** / **weren't** happy.

4 My friends **was** / **were** in the classroom.

5 My sister and I **wasn't** / **weren't** scared.

6 The snowman **was** / **were** a solid.

C Change the underlined word and write *was*, *wasn't*, *were*, or *weren't*.

1 I <u>am</u> very happy. _____was_____

2 It <u>isn't</u> a cold day. _____

3 Lucy <u>is</u> at my house. _____

4 Lucy and I <u>are</u> good friends. _____

5 Her brothers <u>aren't</u> here. _____

6 They <u>are</u> at the playground. _____

D Look at the pictures. Write true sentences using *was*, *wasn't*, *were*, or *weren't*.

1 Kevin / in the park
Kevin wasn't in the park.

2 The water / very cold
_____

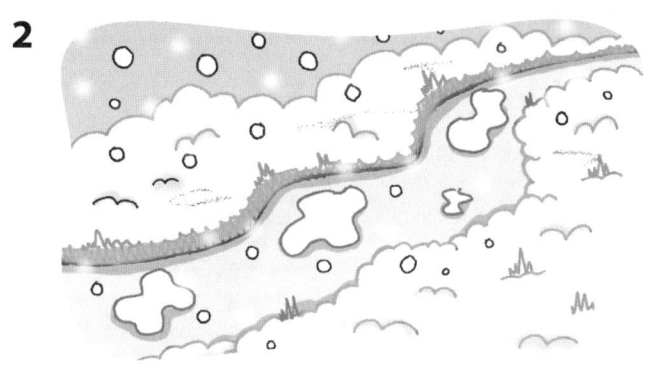

3 Debbie and Ann / sad
_____

4 The sneakers / new
_____

5 The music / loud
_____

6 The cookies / hot
_____

E Complete the sentences about yesterday.

1 I _____ happy.
2 I _____ in the park.
3 I _____ in the classroom.
4 My parents _____ at home.
5 My friends _____ sad.
6 My friends _____ in the park.

Grammar: Simple Past of Verb To Be **Unit 3** 25

Communicate

Words

A Circle the correct words.

1. popcorn / (balloon)

2. candle / icicle

3. candle / kettle

4. icicle / ice pop

5. ice pop / popcorn

6. icicle / kettle

B Complete the chart with words from **A**.

Things We Eat	Things We Don't Eat
1 _____	3 ___balloon___
2 _____	4 _____
	5 _____
	6 _____

Unit 3 Vocabulary: Nouns

Word Study

A Read the sentence and check (✓) the correct picture.

1 I plant a tree in the spring.
   a   b

2 The boys play in the snow.
   a   b

3 Look at the big fish.
   a   b

4 Oh, no! Is that a fly?
   a   b

Writing

A Read about a thing that can change state.

> It's an ice pop. First it was an orange. Oranges are solids. Then it was juice. Juice is a liquid. We freeze it. Now it's an ice pop. It's a solid.

B Choose a thing that can change state and answer the questions about it.

What is it? _____

Is it a liquid / solid / gas? _____

What do you do to it? _____

What is it now? _____

C Now write about that thing.

_____
_____
_____

Student Book page 35

Writing: Words That Can Be Nouns and Verbs Unit 3 **27**

UNIT 4 Get Ready

Words

A Look at the pictures and circle the correct word.

1. (open) / closed

2. mixture / plastic bags

3. sugar / salt

4. cream / salt

5. closed / open

6. pour / freezer

28 Unit 4 *Vocabulary: Food and Mixtures* Student Book page 36

B Look at the picture and write the words.

| cream | mixture | open | ~~freezer~~ | sugar | closed | plastic bag |

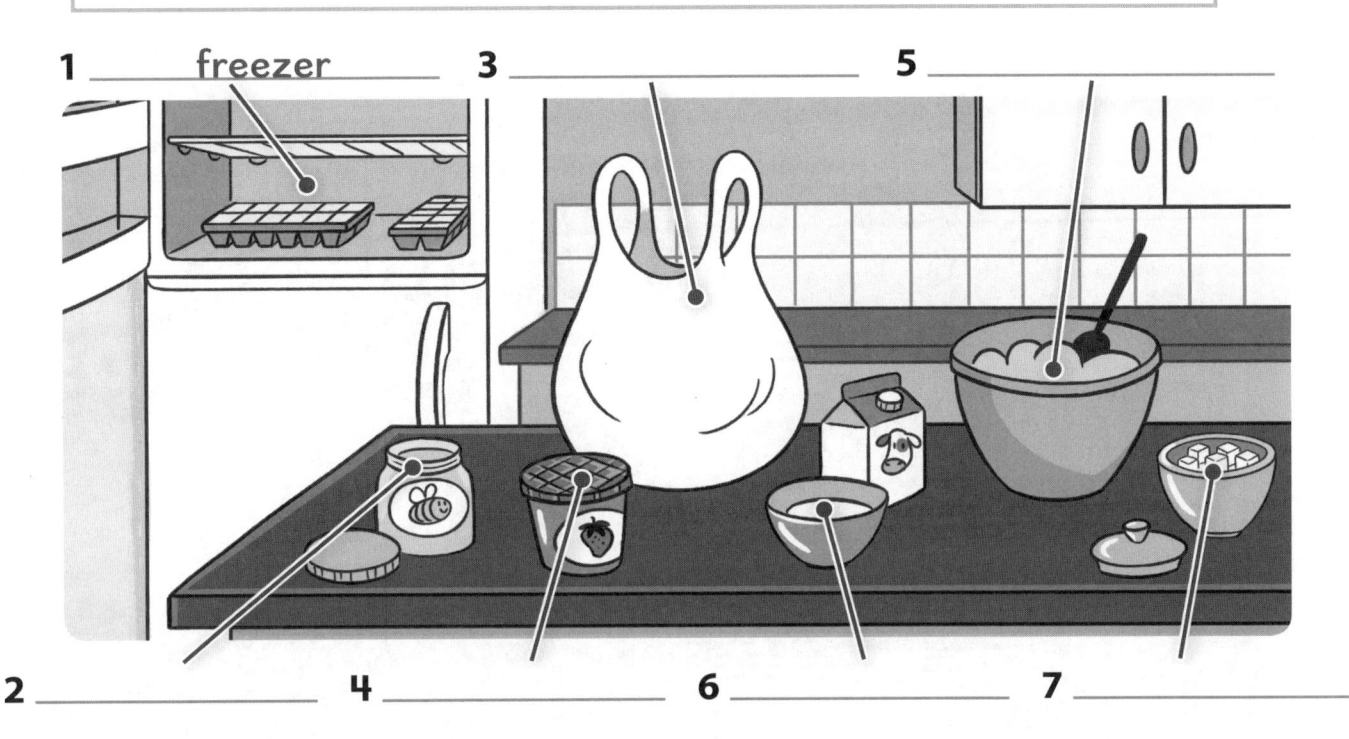

1 _____freezer_____   3 _____   5 _____

2 _____   4 _____   6 _____   7 _____

C Circle *True* or *False*.

1 Sugar is a liquid.	True	(False)
2 I can pour plastic bags.	True	False
3 Plastic bags can be containers.	True	False
4 A door can be open or closed.	True	False
5 We heat things in a freezer.	True	False
6 A mixture has only one thing in it.	True	False

D Complete the sentences.

1 I _____pour_____ milk into a cup.

2 _____, _____, and _____ are all white.

3 Hot chocolate is a _____ of milk, sugar, and chocolate.

4 My mouth and eyes can be _____ or _____.

5 Water changes from a liquid to a solid in the _____.

Vocabulary: Food and Mixtures **Unit 4**

Read

A Read the story quickly. Answer the question.

Two children make ice pops. Why?

_____

Let's Make Ice Pops!

It's summer. David and Lesley play ball in the park. They run a lot and they're hot, so they go home.

Think
They run a lot. / They're hot.
Which is the cause? Which is the effect?

"Can we have some cold soda, Mom?" say David and Lesley. "No, kids," says Mom. "Soda isn't healthy. But I have an idea. Let's make ice pops!" she says. "Get some juice, and add some fruit and a little sugar. Mix it all together, pour the mixture into plastic cups, and put them in the freezer." "OK, Mom," they say.

Think
They make ice pops. / Soda is unhealthy.
Which is the cause? Which is the effect?

David and Lesley eat the cold ice pops. "Were they good?" asks Mom. "Yes, they were delicious!" they say. They're happy.

30 Unit 4 *Reading: Cause and Effect* Student Book page 37

Understand

Comprehension

A What part of the story do you like? Check (✓).

They get hot ☐ They want soda ☐ The ice pops ☐

B Read the causes. Write the effects.

Causes	Effects
1 The children play ball in the park.	a They run a lot.
2 The children are hot.	b
3 Their mother says soda isn't healthy.	c
4 The children eat the ice pops.	d

C Read the story again and answer the questions.

1 Is it a cold day?

   No, it isn't.

2 Where do David and Lesley play ball?

3 Why don't they have soda?

4 How many things are in the ice pop mixture?

5 How does the mixture change in the freezer?

6 Was their mother's idea a good idea? Why? Why not?

Comprehension   Unit 4   31

Grammar in Use

A Study the grammar.

Learn Simple Past of Verb *To Be*

Was	he / she / it	cold?
Were	you	
Were	you / they	

Yes,	he / she / it	**was**.	
	I		
	we / they	**were**.	

No,	he / she / it	**wasn't**.	
	I		
	we / they	**weren't**.	

What		
How	**was**	it?
Where		

It	**was**	an ice pop.
		great.
		in the freezer.

What		
How	**were**	they?
Where		

They	**were**	ice pops.
		great.
		in the freezer.

B Circle the correct words.

1 **(Was)** / Were it a liquid? No, it **(wasn't)** / weren't.

2 **Was** / **Were** you at the museum? Yes. I **was** / **were**.

3 **Was** / **Were** the freezer door open? Yes, it **was** / **were**.

4 **Was** / **Were** you in the library? No, we **wasn't** / **weren't**.

5 **Was** / **Were** Mandy and Kevin scared? Yes, they **was** / **were**.

6 Where **was** / **were** your mother? She **was** / **were** at the department store.

7 **Was** / **Were** Terry at home? No, she **wasn't** / **weren't**.

C Match the questions to the answers.

1. Where was Linda?
2. Was Jenny at the supermarket?
3. Were they friends?
4. How was the soup?
5. Were you and Clare at home?
6. What was in the ice cream mixture?

a. Yes, we were.
b. It was awful.
c. She was at the supermarket.
d. No, she wasn't.
e. Cream, sugar, and eggs.
f. No, they weren't. They were brothers.

D Look at the pictures. Answer the questions.

1. Were the girls in the park?
   Yes, they were.

2. Were the animals fierce?
   _____

3. Was the parade noisy?
   _____

4. Was the party boring?
   _____

E Write the answers.

1. Where were you yesterday?
   _____

2. Where were your parents?
   _____

3. Where was your friend?
   _____

4. Were you happy yesterday?
   _____

5. Was your friend sad?
   _____

6. Were your parents tired?
   _____

Grammar: Simple Past of Verb To Be with Wh- and Yes/No Questions Unit 4 33

Communicate

Words

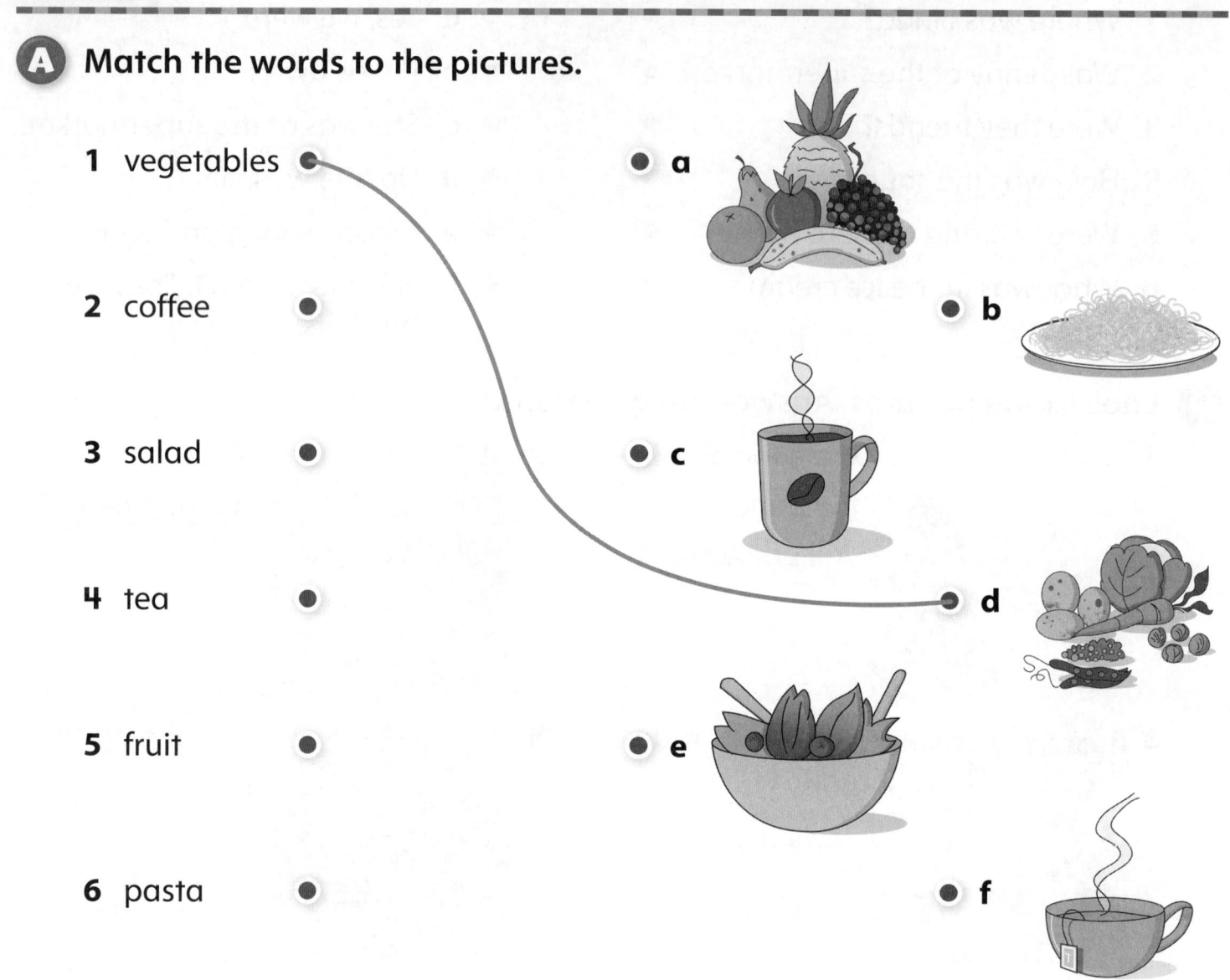

A Match the words to the pictures.

1. vegetables
2. coffee
3. salad
4. tea
5. fruit
6. pasta

a.
b.
c.
d.
e.
f.

B Complete the sentences.

1. Carrots, potatoes, and onions are __vegetables__.
2. People can use black or green leaves and hot water to make _____.
3. A mixture of vegetables is a _____. We don't cook the vegetables.
4. A lot of people drink _____ with cream and sugar.
5. Oranges, apples, mangoes, and peaches are _____.
6. We cook _____ in very hot water so it gets soft. It's usually light yellow or light brown.

34   Unit 4   Vocabulary: Food

Student Book page 42

Writing Study

A Complete the sentences with the short forms.

1 The doors were open. They ____weren't____ closed.
2 Mary and her sister are happy. They _____ sad.
3 Ice is a solid. It _____ a gas.
4 The salad was cold. It _____ hot.

Writing

A Read about Jimmy's favorite food mixture.

> My favorite food mixture is soup. My mother puts chicken, onions, carrots, and potatoes in a big pot. She puts in water and salt. She cooks it. We eat the soup. It's great!

B Answer the questions about your favorite food or drink mixture.

What's your favorite mixture? _____
What things are in the mixture? _____
_____

What do you do to the mixture?
_____

Do you eat or drink it? _____
How is it? _____

C Now write about your favorite food mixture.

_____
_____
_____
_____
_____
_____

What have you learned?

Review

A Check (✓) the things we can eat or drink.

1. ✓ cream
2. ☐ gas
3. ☐ ice pop
4. ☐ coffee
5. ☐ balloon
6. ☐ sugar
7. ☐ pasta
8. ☐ kettle
9. ☐ soup

B Complete the sentences.

| flow | melt | freeze | pour | mixture | heat |

1 Liquids can _____, but solids can't.

2 When we _____ water, some of it can change to steam.

3 Soup is a _____ of liquids and solids.

4 When we _____ liquids, they change to solids.

5 We can _____ a liquid, but not a solid or a gas.

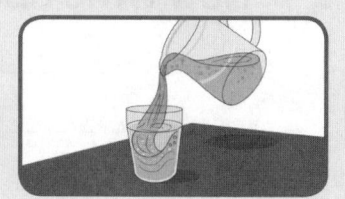

6 Ice pops _____ when we don't put them in the freezer.

BIG QUESTION 2
How do things change?

36

C Circle the correct words.

1 The ice pops **wasn't** / **(weren't)** in the freezer.
2 **Was** / **Were** you at the library?
3 His cousins **was** / **were** very happy.
4 It **was** / **were** a solid but now it's a liquid.
5 The guitar **wasn't** / **weren't** loud.
6 Where **was** / **were** Wendy and Andy?
7 **Was** / **Were** your mother at the supermarket?
8 How **was** / **were** the cookies?

D Complete the sentences. Write *was*, *were*, *wasn't*, or *weren't*.

1 _____Were_____ the girls in the restaurant?
No, they _____. They _____ in the movie theater.
2 How _____ the pasta?
It _____ awful.
3 _____ Kevin happy?
Yes, he _____.
4 Where _____ the ice pops?
They _____ in the freezer.
5 _____ you at the beach?
No, I _____. I _____ at the park.
6 It's a liquid now. What _____ it?
It _____ a solid, ice cream.

E Circle the short forms. Then underline the words that can be nouns and verbs.

1 There (wasn't) a lot of snow on the tree.
2 The plant isn't very big.
3 There weren't any fish in the pond.
4 The fly isn't brown. It's black.

Review 37

BIG QUESTION 3

How are things different now from long ago?

Think about the Big Question. Write.

What do you know?
_____
_____
_____
_____
_____
_____
_____

What do you want to know?
_____
_____
_____
_____
_____
_____
_____

UNIT 5 Get Ready

Words

A Number the words.

_4_ travel	___ news	___ text message
___ radio	___ e-mail	___ communication

1.
2.
3.
4.
5.
6.

Vocabulary: Travel, Communication, and News

Student Book page 48

B Write the words. Then match the words to the pictures.

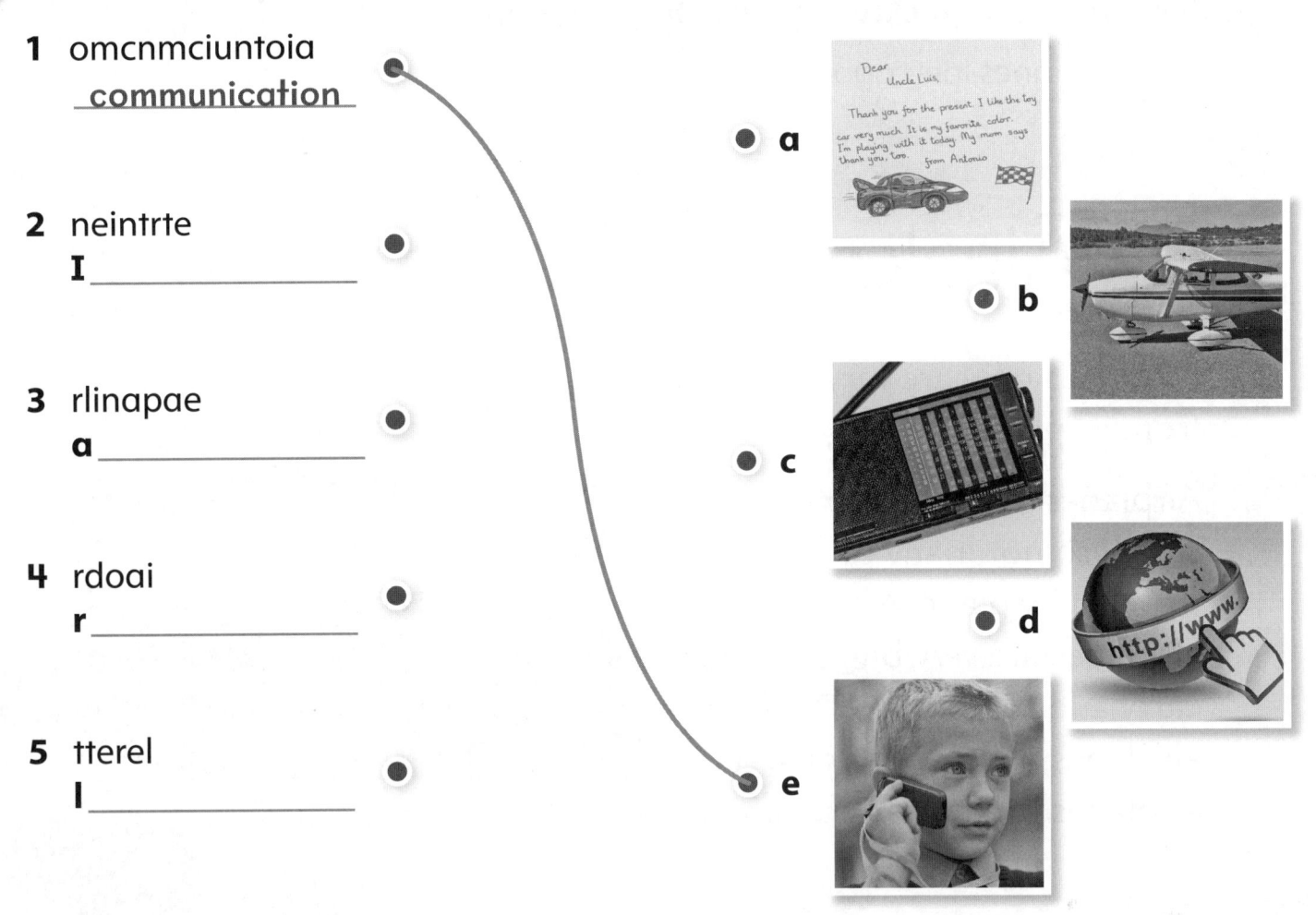

1 omcnmciuntoia
   communication

2 neintrte
   I_____

3 rlinapae
   a_____

4 rdoai
   r_____

5 tterel
   l_____

a
b
c
d
e

C Circle the correct words.

1 Sam sometimes listens to music on the **radio** / **news**.

2 Her friend likes to play games on **e-mail** / **the Internet**.

3 **Travel** / **Communication** by airplane is fun.

4 My teacher sends us **text messages** / **Internet** about our homework.

D Read the clues. Write the words.

1 This flies in the sky. airplane

2 We write this with a pen or a pencil. _____

3 This is like a letter, but we send it on a computer. _____

4 This message on a phone usually has only few words. _____

5 We can listen to the news on this. We can't see pictures on it. _____

Vocabulary: Travel, Communication, and News   Unit 5   **39**

Read

A Read the text quickly. Answer the question.

Were airplanes long ago safe?

Airplanes Then and Now

Airplanes now are very different from airplanes long ago.

Airplanes long ago were very small, so not many people traveled by plane. Now airplanes are very big, and they carry a lot of people. The first airplanes were dangerous, but airplanes today are very safe.

The first airplanes were also slow and didn't fly very far. Airplanes now are very fast and can fly to places far away. They carry people, letters, food, and other thing to many places around the world.

Think

What's the main idea?
What's a detail of the main idea?

Understand

Comprehension

A What part of the text do you like? Check (✓).

The first airplanes ☐   Airplanes today ☐   Airplanes carry things ☐

B Write the main idea of the text and three details.

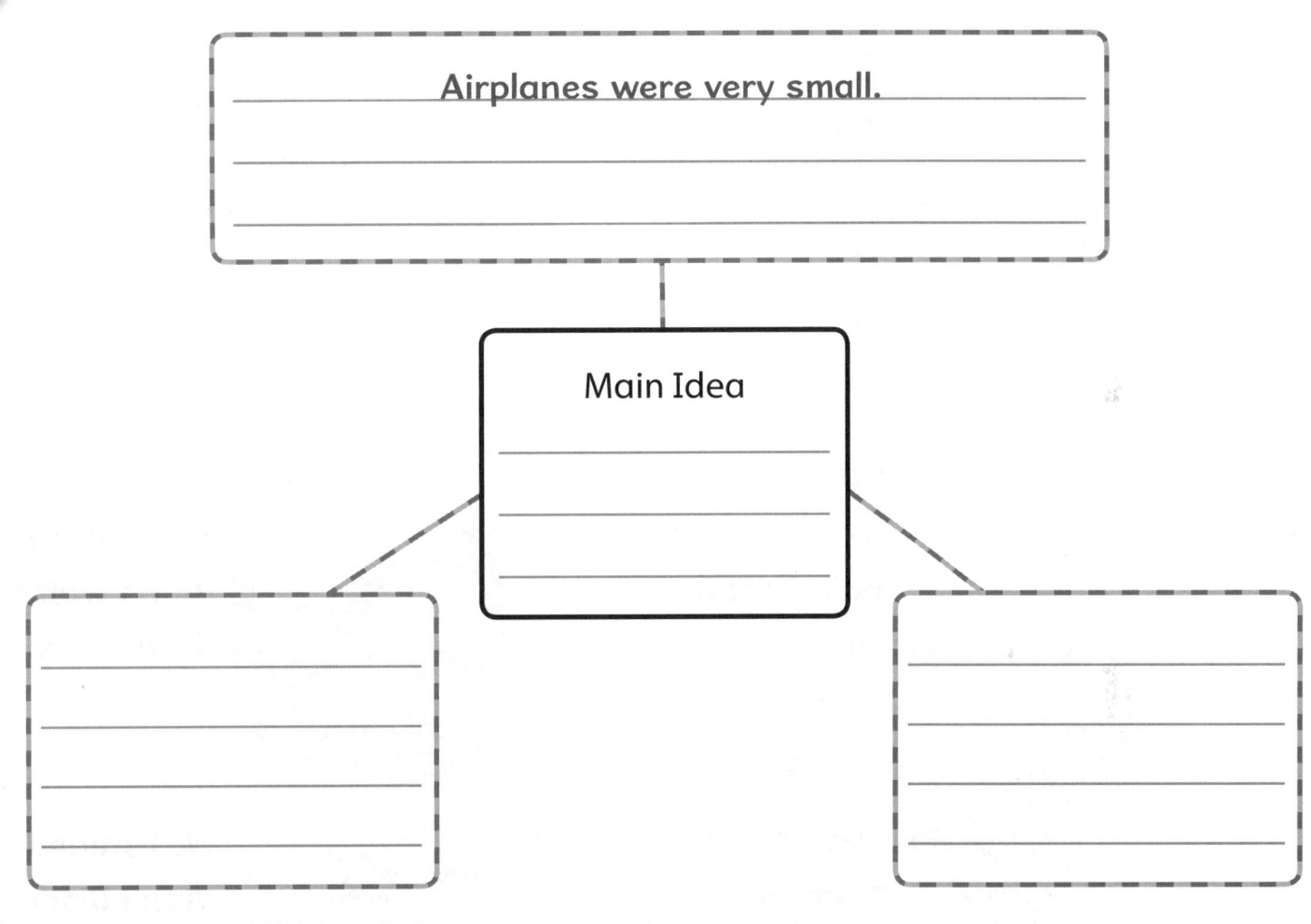

Airplanes were very small.

Main Idea

C Circle *True* or *False*.

1 Airplanes long ago carried a lot of people.   True   (False)
2 Long ago it was safe to travel by plane.   True   False
3 Today travel by airplane from one city to another city is fast.   True   False
4 Long ago airplanes carried food and letters to places far away.   True   False
5 Long ago people traveled around the world by airplane.   True   False

Grammar in Use

A Study the grammar.

Learn Simple Past of Regular Verbs

Now		
I you we they	**travel** **don't travel**	by car.
he she it	**travels** **doesn't travel**	

Then		
I you he she it we they	**traveled** **didn't travel**	by car.

B Circle the correct words.

1. My grandmother **mail** / **(mailed)** letters to her friends a long time ago.

2. Mary **watched** / **didn't watch** the news on TV.

3. They **travel** / **traveled** to Italy by ship long ago.

4. We **listened** / **didn't listen** to the radio.

5. Tim and Kate **didn't walk** / **walked** to school.

6. I **cleaned** / **didn't clean** my room.

42   Unit 5   *Grammar: Simple Past Regular Verbs*   Student Book page 53

C Complete the sentences with the past tense.

> walk   talk   watch   ~~mail~~   send   listen   travel

A long time ago people ___mailed___₁ letters to communicate. They didn't

_____₂ e-mails. They didn't _____₃ by car. They _____₄ or traveled

by horse and cart. People didn't _____₅ the news on TV. They _____₆

to the radio and they sometimes _____₇ to each other to get news.

D Use the words to make sentences in the past tense.

1 My friend and I / not use / e-mail.
   My friend and I didn't use e-mail.

2 My sister / talk / to her friend / on the phone.
   _____

3 Olivia / not watch / TV / with her brother.
   _____

4 We / play / a game / in the park.
   _____

E What did you do yesterday? Write a (✓) or a (✗).
Then write true sentences.

1 walk to school	___	I _____.
2 play a game	___	_____.
3 clean my room	___	_____.
4 watch TV	___	_____.
5 use email	___	_____.
6 listen to music	___	_____.

Grammar: Simple Past Regular Verbs   Unit 5   43

Communicate

Words

A Complete the chart.

| cable car | horse | truck | boat | bus | motorcycle |

	It Has Wheels.		It Doesn't Have Wheels.
1	cable car	5	_____
2	_____	6	_____
3	_____		
4	_____		

B Look at the pictures and complete the puzzles with the words from **A**.

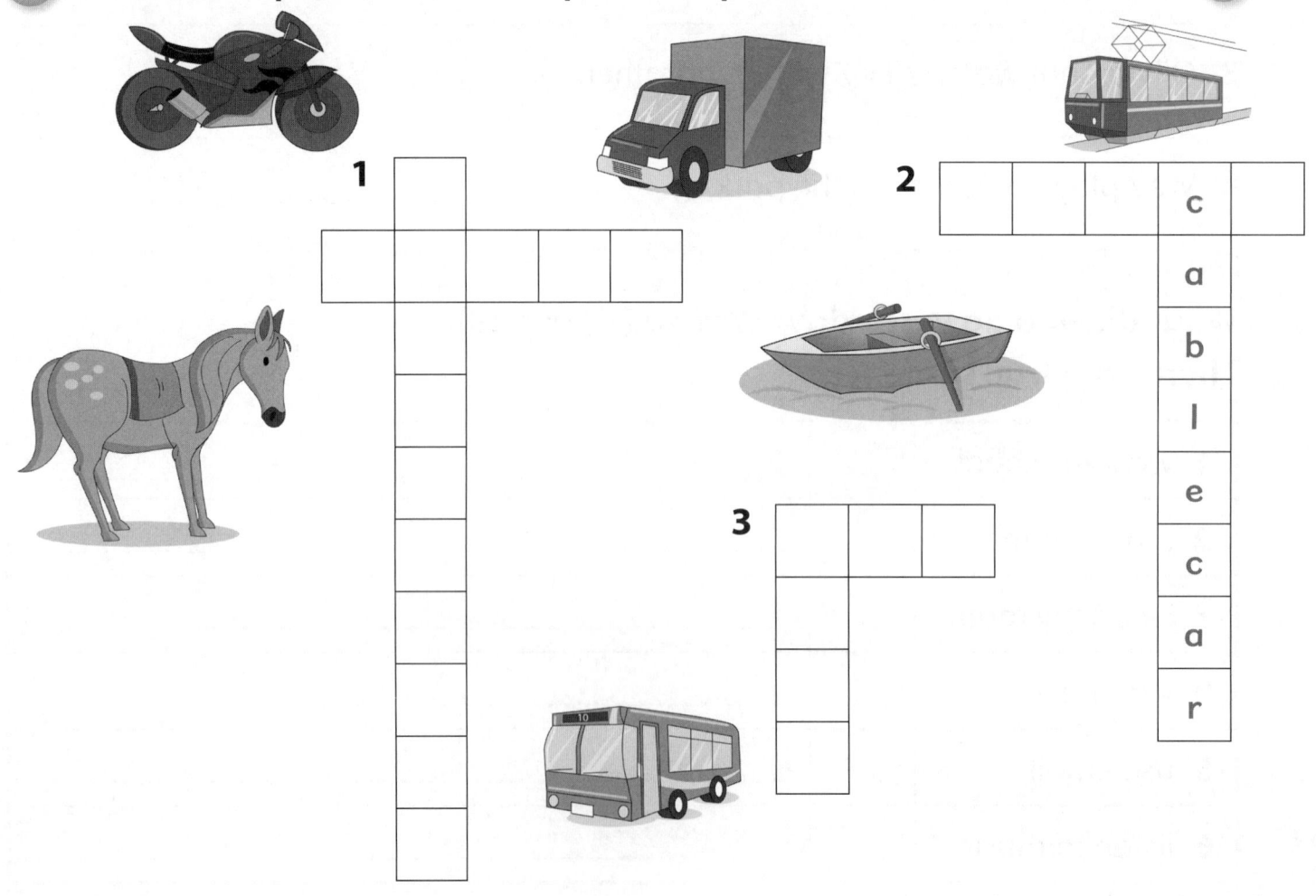

2 down: c a b l e c a r

44   Unit 5   *Vocabulary: Transport*   Student Book page 54

Word Study

A Write the words in alphabetical order.

| bicycle | ~~bake~~ | bench | body | bus | bird | beach | beetle |

1. _____bake_____
2. _____
3. _____
4. _____
5. _____
6. _____
7. _____
8. _____

Writing

A Read about communication long ago and now.

> Long ago people mailed letters to each other. Letters traveled very slowly and communication was slow. Now people talk or text on the phone and send e-mails. Communication is very fast.

B Think about something that was different in the past. Answer the questions about it.

What did people do long ago? _____

How was it then? _____

What do they do now? _____

How is it now? _____

C Now write about it.

_____
_____
_____
_____

UNIT 6 Get Ready

Words

A Circle the action words.

(arrive) ask check

clerk crowded enter poor

sick visit

B Write the words from A under the correct picture.

1. sick
2. _____ 
3. _____ 
4. _____ 
5. _____ 
6. _____

46 Unit 6 *Vocabulary: Travel Nouns and Verbs* Student Book page 56

C Match the beginnings of the sentences to the ends.

1 A lot of people were on the boat. It was — d
2 He works in a supermarket. He's a
3 My body is hot and I'm tired. I'm
4 He didn't have a lot of money. He was
5 He mailed a letter to his friend. It
6 Her grandparents live in Boston. She often

a poor.
b sick.
c visits them.
d crowded.
e clerk.
f arrived a month later.

D Circle the odd one out.

1 **clerk:**   department store   movie theatre   (park)   drugstore
2 **visit:**   friends   berries   cousins   grandparents
3 **crowded:**   drugstore   boat   cable car   horse
4 **ask:**   doctor   police officer   radio   teacher

E Complete the text with the correct words.

crowded   ask   ~~visit~~   walk   checks   arrive

It's Sunday. My parents ____visit____ my sister, Maggie, in London. She has
                              1
a new apartment. They travel to London by train. The train is _____.
                                                                    2
A man on the train _____ their
                          3
tickets. They _____ in London
                    4
in the afternoon. They _____
                              5
a police officer where the apartment
is, then they _____ to it.
                    6
They see my sister, and they're happy.

Vocabulary: Travel Nouns and Verbs Unit 6 47

Read

A Read the story quickly. Answer the question.

Why did Wendy's great grandma go to New York?

_____

My Grandma's Grandparents

"How did your grandparents meet, Grandma?" asks Wendy.

"My Grandpa Charles and Grandma Betty were neighbors and then classmates," says Grandma.

"In New York?" asks Wendy.

"Oh, no, Wendy. They lived in England," says Grandma. "When Grandpa Charles was 20, he traveled to New York, but Grandma Betty stayed in England. They mailed letters to each other, but the letters arrived one month later! Grandma Betty missed Grandpa Charles, so she traveled from England by ship, and she arrived in New York after seven days. The trip was awful."

"Wow! Now people often fly between England and New York, and they get there on the same day!" says Wendy.

Understand

Comprehension

A What part of the story do you like? Check (✓).

New York ☐   England ☐   The ship ☐

B Put the events in the correct order. Write the numbers.

___ Grandpa Charles traveled to New York.
___ Grandma Betty arrived in New York.
_1_ Grandpa Charles and Grandma Betty lived in England.
___ Grandma Betty traveled to New York by ship.

C Read the questions. Check (✓) the correct answers.

1 Grandpa Charles and Grandma Betty were …
   a ✓ neighbors.
   b ☐ friends.

2 When they were children Grandpa Charles and Grandma Betty lived in …
   a ☐ New York.
   b ☐ England.

3 Grandma Betty …
   a ☐ mailed letters to Grandpa Charles.
   b ☐ used the radio to talk to Grandpa Charles.

4 On the ship to New York, Grandma Betty was …
   a ☐ happy.
   b ☐ not happy.

5 The trip to New York was …
   a ☐ long.
   b ☐ interesting.

Comprehension Unit 6 49

Grammar in Use

A Study the grammar.

Learn Simple Past of Regular Verbs

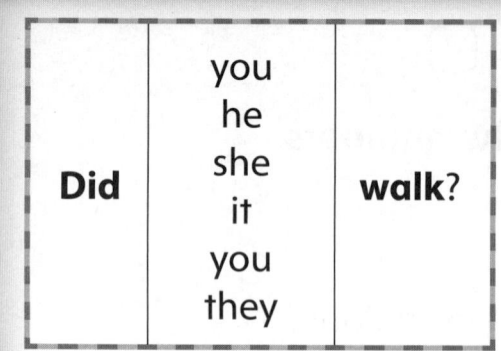

| Did | you / he / she / it / you / they | walk? |

| Yes, | I / he / she / it / we / they | **did**. |
| No, | | **didn't**. |

| Where / What / How | **did** | you / he / she / it / you / they | **live** / **do?** / **travel?** |

I / He / She / It / We / They	**lived** in New York.
	played ball.
	traveled by ship.

B Match the questions to the answers.

1. What did Billy do?
2. What did you do?
3. Did Maya travel to Italy?
4. How did Annie travel?
5. Did Mark watch TV?
6. What did you play?
7. Where did Jose and Pete walk to?
8. Did Malik and Pete live in Chicago?

a. She traveled by bus.
b. He baked cookies.
c. We played basketball.
d. No, he didn't. He played a game.
e. They walked to the playground.
f. Yes, they did.
g. I cleaned my room.
h. Yes, she did.

1 → b

C Look at the pictures and answer the questions.

1 Did Lucy and Bill walk home?
Yes, they did.

2 Did Jenny watch TV?
_____

3 What did they do?
_____

4 Did Jack talk to his mother?
_____

5 Where did her grandmother live?
_____

6 What did she cook?
_____

D Write about what you did yesterday.

1 Did you visit your aunt yesterday?
_____

2 Where did you walk to?
_____

3 What game or sport did you play?
_____

4 What TV programme did you watch?
_____

Grammar: Simple Past Regular Verbs with Wh- and Yes/No Questions **Unit 6** **51**

Communicate

Words

A Look at the picture and number the words.

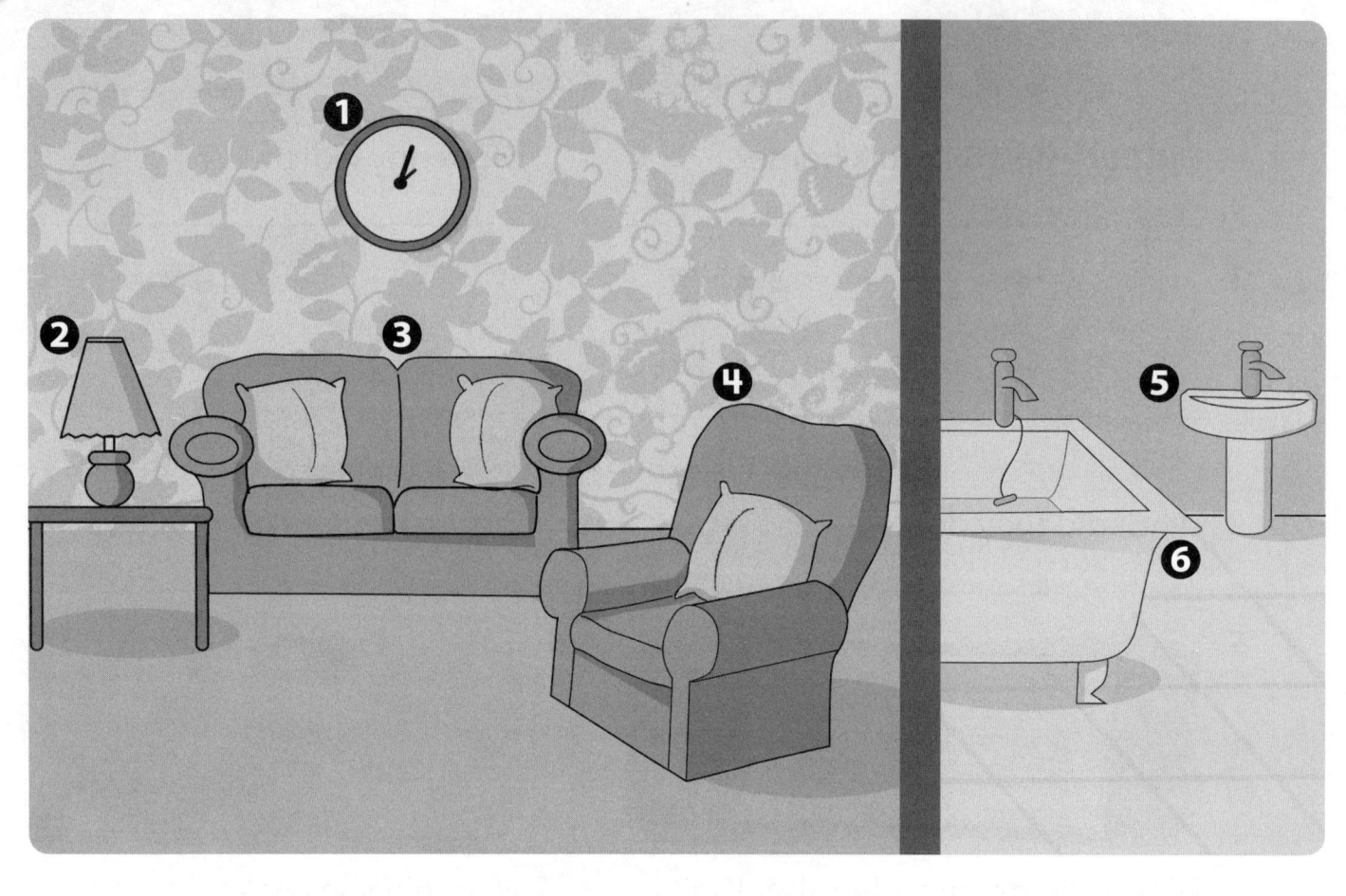

| _5_ sink | ___ chair | ___ lamp | ___ clock | ___ bathtub | ___ couch |

B Complete the chart.

Things We Sit On or In	Things We Don't Sit On or In
1 _____	4 _____ sink _____
2 _____	5 _____
3 _____	6 _____

52 Unit 6   *Vocabulary: Furniture*   Student Book page 62

Writing Study

A Check (✓) the verbs in the past tense.

1. ✓ asked
2. ☐ travel
3. ☐ mailed
4. ☐ cooked
5. ☐ talk
6. ☐ clean

B Write the past tense of these verbs.

1. listen _listened_
2. mail _____
3. check _____
4. watch _____
5. print _____
6. enter _____
7. walk _____
8. visit _____
9. bake _____

Writing

A Read about how people traveled long ago and how they travel now.

> Some people traveled from New York to New Jersey by horse long ago. Sometimes it was hot or cold outside. It was difficult in the rain and snow. It was slow, too. Now people travel by car. It's easy and fast.

B Think about traveling to a place 100 years ago and traveling to that place now. Answer the questions.

How did people travel long ago? _____
How was the trip long ago? _____
How do people travel now? _____
How is the trip now? _____

C Now write about traveling to that place long ago and now.

_____
_____
_____
_____
_____
_____

Writing: Adding -ed To Some Verbs **Unit 6** 53

What have you learned?

Review

A Circle the odd one out.

1. poor   crowded   (trip)
2. boat   truck   bus
3. lamp   sink   clock
4. news   e-mail   text message
5. sink   bathtub   clerk
6. ask   check   Internet
7. enter   arrive   couch
8. couch   radio   chair

B Find and circle six words. Then write them.

t	r	u	c	k	g	h	z
r	a	r	r	i	v	e	t
a	f	h	b	a	q	z	t
v	s	c	o	u	c	h	l
e	i	p	u	r	j	k	e
l	n	r	c	m	e	y	z
g	k	x	d	i	o	r	h
w	b	a	t	h	t	u	b

1. _truck_
2. _____
3. _____
4. _____
5. _____
6. _____

BIG QUESTION 3

How are things different now from long ago?

54

C Look at the pictures. Write *T* (*True*) or *F* (*False*).

1. She traveled to New York by ship. _F_
2. She didn't bake an apple pie. ___
3. She mailed a letter to her friend. ___
4. He didn't walk to school. ___

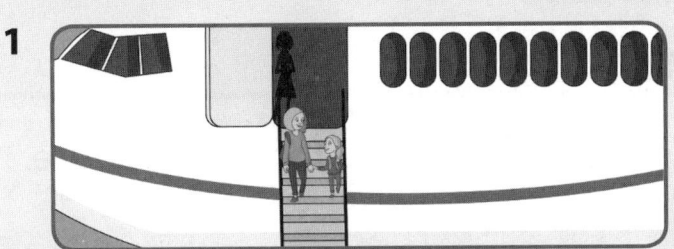

D Look at the chart. Write the questions and answers.

	Walk To the Park	Bake a Cake	Travel By Ship	Watch a Movie
Stevie	✓	✗	✗	✓
Rosie	✗	✓	✓	✗

1. Stevie / travel by ship? <u>Did Stevie travel by ship? No, he didn't.</u>

2. Where / Stevie / walk to? _____

3. Rosie / watch a movie? _____

4. What / Stevie / watch? _____

5. What / Rosie / bake? _____

6. Stevie / bake a cake? _____

Review 55

7 Get Ready

BIG QUESTION 4

When do we use subtraction?

Think about the Big Question. Write.

What do you know?

_____
_____
_____
_____
_____
_____

What do you want to know?

_____
_____
_____
_____
_____
_____

Words

A Circle the correct word for each picture.

1. 
take away
~~test score~~ (circled)
row

2. 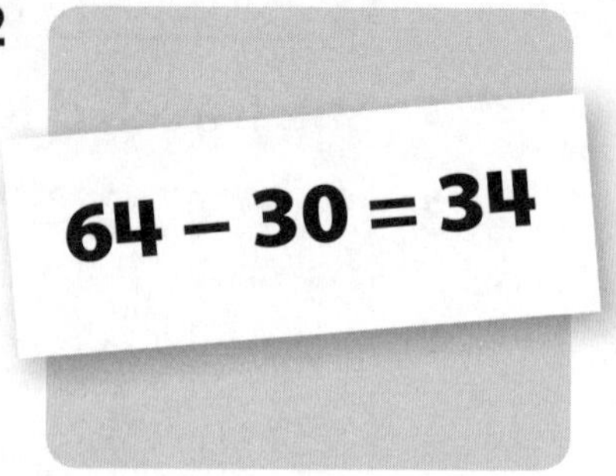
subtraction
take away
column

3. 
left
row
take away

4. 
column
left
test score

5. 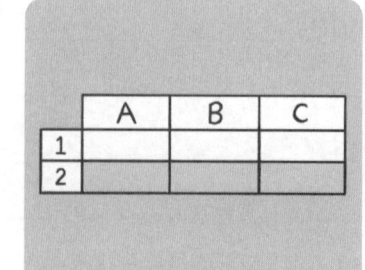
subtraction
column
row

6. 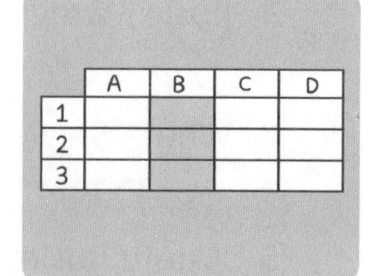
take away
column
minus sign

56   Unit 7   Vocabulary: Math   Student Book page 68

B Write the words.

single-digit number   double-digit number   minus sign   ~~row~~   column

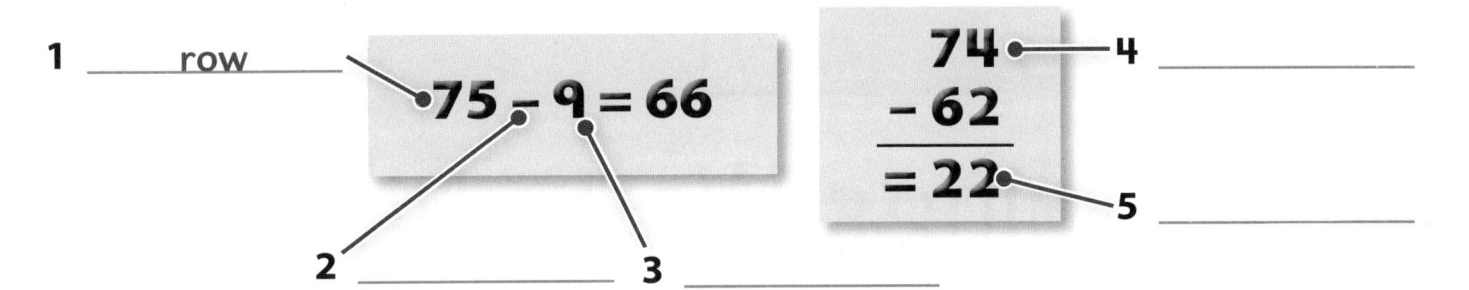

1 __row__

75 − 9 = 66

2 _____   3 _____

74 — 4 _____
− 62
= 22 — 5 _____

C Match the beginnings of the sentences to the ends.

1 Twenty-six is — d

2 When we subtract

3 All subtraction problems

4 I have seven apples. I eat four apples. I have — b

a have a minus sign

b three apples left.

c we take things away.

d a double-digit number.

D Look at the table. Complete the sentences.

	1	2	3	4	5	6	7
A	64	−	6	=	58		92
B						−	49
C						=	43

1 A2 is a __minus sign__

2 A1 to A5 is a _____ problem in a _____.

3 A7 to C7 is a _____ problem in a _____.

4 A2 tells me to _____ 6 from 64.

5 C7 tells me that 43 are _____.

6 A3 is a _____ number.

7 B7 is a _____ number.

Vocabulary: Math   Unit 7   57

Read

A Read the text quickly. Answer the question.

How much time does Kabir have left?

_____

Things We Subtract

¹ We use subtraction every day. When we buy things, we subtract to find out how much money we have left. Look at this example. Rosa had ten dollars. She bought a book for four dollars. She takes away four from ten and finds out she has six dollars left.

² We can subtract time too. For example, Kabir's class starts in forty-five minutes. He can walk to class in thirty minutes. He subtracts thirty from forty-five and finds out he has fifteen minutes left. Hurry up, Kabir!

Think
Reread this part slowly. Do you understand it?

³ You try this one. Ms. Zerilli is baking a pie. She put the pie in the oven ten minutes ago. It needs to bake for fifty minutes. How much time does the pie still need to bake?

Understand

Comprehension

A What part of the text do you like? Check (✓).

Rosa ☐   Kabir ☐   Ms Zerilli ☐

B Look at the word problem in paragraphs 1–3. Write the number problems.

Paragraph 1

10 – 4 = 6

Paragraph 2

Paragraph 3

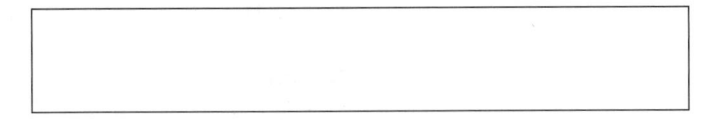

C Circle *True* or *False*. Correct the false statements.

1 When we buy things, we subtract to find out how much money we can have.

   True   (False)

   We subtract to find out how much money we have left.

2 After Rosa buys the book, she has six dollars to spend.

   True   False

3 Kabir needs to hurry because he has fifteen minutes to get to class.

   True   False

4 Ms. Zerilli's pie still needs to bake for ten minutes.

   True   False

Grammar in Use

A Study the grammar.

Learn Simple Past of Irregular Verbs

| I you he she it we they | ate | an apple. |
| | didn't eat | |

B Write the past tense.

1 buy   bought
2 have   _____
3 go   _____
4 drink _____
5 eat   _____
6 see   _____
7 fly   _____
8 sell   _____
9 give   _____

C Match the beginnings of the sentences to the ends.

1  Lisa didn't …   a buy new sneakers.
2 Malik …   b ate three cookies.
3 Leela …   c eat a sandwich.
4 Ian didn't …   d bought a new jacket.

60 Unit 7 *Grammar: Simple Past Irregular Verbs in Negative Statements*   Student Book page 73

D Read these sentences about yesterday and circle the correct words.

1 My mother and father **drink** / **(drank)** coffee.

2 I didn't **see** / **saw** you in the park.

3 The girls **have** / **had** cookies and fruit in their backpacks.

4 Jack and Betsy didn't **go** / **went** to school.

E Complete the subtraction problems with the past tense. Then solve the problems.

| go   fly   eat   sell   ~~buy~~ |

1 Thomas had twenty-five dollars. He ___bought___ a pin for five dollars. How many dollars were left? ___twenty___

2 Yoko had thirty-two cookies. She _____ six. How many cookies were left? _____

3 The man had forty-eight balloons. He _____ thirty-three. How many balloons were left? _____

4 Joe saw fifty-one birds in a tree. Forty-six birds _____ away. How many birds were left? _____

5 Eighteen boys played ball on the playground. Ten _____ home. How many boys were left? _____

F What did you do yesterday? Write a (✓) or a (✗). Then write sentences.

1 eat pasta	___	I _____.
2 buy a new T-shirt	___	_____.
3 drink soda	___	_____.
4 see my teacher	___	_____.

Grammar: Simple Past Irregular Verbs in Negative Statements   **Unit 7**

Communicate

Words

A Match the words to the pictures.

1 dirty

2 hungry

3 clean

4 thirsty

a

b

c

d

B Complete the sentences.

1 Billy wants a sandwich and fruit. He's very _____hungry_____.

2 It's late, and Judy wants to go to bed. She's _____.

3 Johnny washed his car. It's _____.

4 Lisa wants cold water. She's _____.

Word Study

A Circle the word with a different amount of syllables.

1. double   crowded   thirsty   (full)
2. score   row   number   take
3. hungry   twenty   many   Internet
4. thirsty   dirty   check   mixture
5. gills   amphibian   skin   fur
6. sleepy   hungry   thirsty   dangerous

Writing

A Read this subtraction problem.

> There were twenty-five icicles on the house.
> The sun came out and melted nineteen icicles.
> How many icicles were left?

B Think about an interesting subtraction problem and answer the questions.

How many things were there? _____
What happened to the things? _____
How many things were left? _____

C Now write the subtraction problem in words.

_____
_____
_____
_____

UNIT 8 Get Ready

Words

A Draw a line and join the action words in order.

let go	pasta	dirty	baker	visit
jar	hide	column	dig up	hungry
bored	thirsty	steal	mixture	greedy

What letter do the lines form? Write the letter: _____

B Look at the pictures and write the words.

| let go | steal | ~~dig up~~ | hide | jar | greedy | bored | baker | cook |

1. dig up
2. _____  
3. _____ 
4. _____ 
5. _____ 
6. _____ 
7. _____ 
8. _____ 
9. _____

C Match the sentences to the words.

1 Someone who makes bread, cakes, and cookies.   a bored
2 You have a lot of things, but you want more things.   b baker
3 Someone who makes food in restaurants and hotels.   c jar
4 We can put things in this.   d cook
5 You don't have interesting things to do.   e greedy

D Circle the correct words, then write the words to complete the sentences.

1 The farmer ____digs up____ the potatoes with his hands.
  a visits
  b hides
  c (digs up)

2 My mom puts some sugar into an empty _____.
  a cream
  b chair
  c jar

3 A _____ makes pasta, salad, soup, and other things to eat.
  a doctor
  b cook
  c baker

4 It's a rainy day. Rosie can't play outside. She's _____.
  a greedy
  b bored
  c fierce

5 It isn't good to _____ things from other people.
  a ask
  b check
  c steal

Vocabulary: People Nouns and Verbs   Unit 8   65

Read

A Read the story quickly. Answer the question.

What does Sammy Squirrel dig up?

_____

Sammy's Missing Acorns

It was fall. "Get ready for winter!" said Sammy Squirrel to his lazy cousin. "You work too hard!" said Lazy Larry. "No, I don't," said Sammy, and he ran off to dig up more acorns.

When he got back home he said, "Now I have 100 acorns. I have enough for winter." Sammy counted the acorns and saw that 10 were missing! The next day, another 20 acorns were missing, and the next day, another 15 acorns were missing!

Sammy ran to Lazy Larry's house. "Someone stole my acorns! I'm not happy!" "Really?" said Larry. "That's awful!". Sammy looked around Lazy Larry's house and saw acorns all over. He counted 45 acorns! Who stole Sammy's acorns? Larry did! Sammy wasn't happy. Larry apologized and returned 45 acorns to Sammy.

Understand

Comprehension

A What part of the story do you like? Check (✓).

Sammy Squirrel ☐   Lazy Larry ☐   The end of the story ☐

B Number the sentences in the correct order. Then write B (beginning) for one sentence, M (middle) for four sentences, and E (end) for one sentence.

___ Sammy saw acorns all over Lazy Larry's house. ___
___ Sammy wasn't happy with Larry. ___
___ There were acorns missing from Sammy's house. ___
___ Sammy ran off to dig up more acorns. ___
_1_ "Get ready for winter!" said Sammy Squirrel to Lazy Larry. _B_
___ Larry gave back the acorns. ___

C Answer the questions.

1. Do Sammy Squirrel and Lazy Larry live in the same house?
   No, they don't.

2. How many acorns did Sammy Squirrel have for winter?
   _____

3. How does Lazy Larry get acorns?
   _____

4. Is Sammy Squirrel smart? Why/Why not?
   _____
   _____

5. Is Lazy Larry smart? Why/Why not?
   _____
   _____

6. Why did Lazy Larry give acorns to Sammy Squirrel?
   _____
   _____

Grammar in Use

A Study the grammar

Learn Simple Past of Irregular Verbs

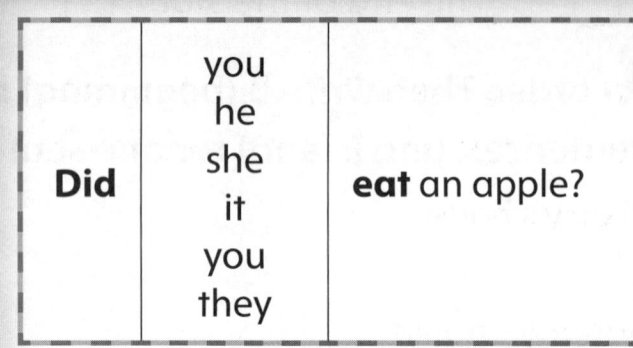

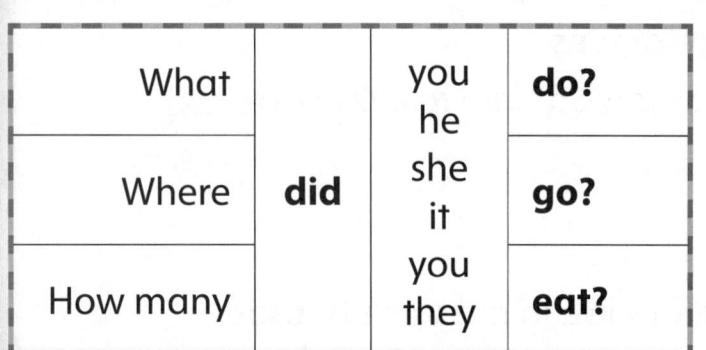

Did	you / he / she / it / you / they	**eat** an apple?

Yes,	I / he / she / it / we / they	**did.**
No,		**didn't.**

What		you	**do?**
Where	did	he / she / it	**go?**
How many		you / they	**eat?**

I / He / She / It / We / They	**drank** some water.
	went to the park.
	ate three.

B Circle the correct words.

1. Did the boys (**run**) / **ran** to the playground?
   (**Yes**) / **No**, they did.

2. **What** / **Where** did Paul and Jack drink?
   They **drink** / **drank** orange juice.

3. Did the dog **steal** / **stole** a sausage?
   No, it **did** / **didn't**.

4. **How many** / **What** balloons did you buy?
   We **buy** / **bought** fourteen balloons.

5. Did Emily **make** / **made** a sandwich?
   Yes / **No**, she didn't.

C Look at the pictures and answer the questions.

1 Where did Mark and his father go?
   They went to the bakery.

2 Did Pedro have three kites?
   _____

3 How many ice pops did the girls eat?
   _____

4 Did the cook make pasta?
   _____

D Match the questions to the correct answers.

1 What did the monkey steal? — b
2 Did Aisha go to the candy store?
3 Did the rabbit dig up a carrot?
4 How many sausages did the dog eat?

a It ate two.
b It stole a banana.
c Yes, it did.
d No, she didn't.

E What did you do yesterday? Answer the questions.

1 Did you eat candy?
   _____

2 Did you make a sandwich?
   _____

3 How many friends did you see?
   _____

4 Did you drink milk?
   _____

Grammar: Simple Past Irregular Verbs with Wh- and Yes/No Questions **Unit 8**

Communicate

Words

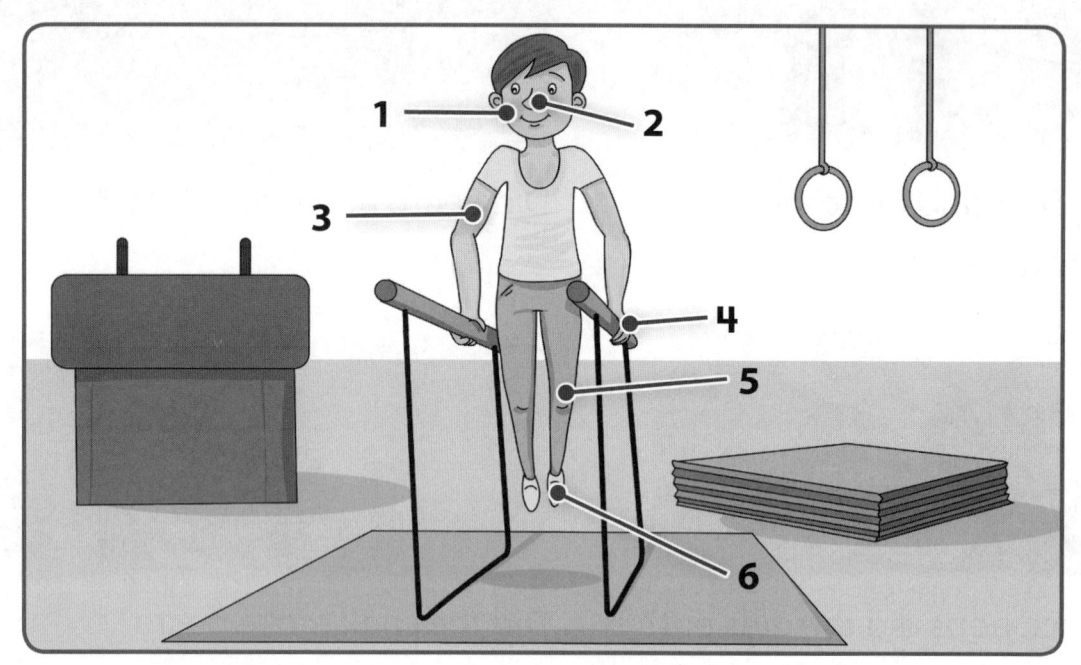

A Look at the picture and number the words.

___ arm
___ knee
_1_ face
___ hand
___ foot
___ nose

B Read the sentences and write the letters.

a a monkey   b a goldfish   c a horse   d a spider   e ~~an eagle~~

1 This animal has two legs, two feet, and a face. It doesn't have arms or hands. What is it? _e_

2 This animal doesn't have legs, knees, arms, hands, or feet. What is it? ___

3 This animal doesn't have hands, arms, or a nose, but it has eight legs. What is it? ___

4 This animal has two arms, two hands, two legs, two feet, and a very cute face. What is it? ___

5 This animal has four legs, knees, and feet. It has a big face. It doesn't have arms or hands. What is it? ___

70   Unit 8   Vocabulary: Body   Student Book page 82

Writing Study

A Write the short forms

1. cannot   __can't__
2. should not   _____
3. do not   _____
4. does not   _____
5. did not   _____
6. is not   _____

B Circle the possible short forms, then write them.

1. The squirrel (did not) hide the acorns.   __didn't__
2. You should not talk in the library.   _____
3. My sister does not want candy.   _____
4. The monkey cannot swim.   _____

Writing

A Read about three things Tony did last night.

> I read a book. It was interesting. I watched TV with my brother and sister. Then I went to bed.

B Complete the chart about three things you did last night.

1. _____
2. _____
3. _____

C Now write about the things you did last night.

_____
_____
_____
_____

Student Book page 83   Writing: Contractions   Unit 8   71

What have you learned?

Review

A Complete the sentences.

> tired   greedy   stole   single-digit   row
> column   dirty   double-digit   ~~subtraction~~

1. $9 - 5 = 4$

   This is a _subtraction_ problem. The numbers are in a _____. Nine and five are _____ numbers.

2. $$\begin{array}{r} 58 \\ -50 \\ \hline 8 \end{array}$$

   This problem is in a _____. Fifty-eight and fifty are _____ numbers.

3. Look at the cat. It's _____ and _____.

4. The _____ monkey _____ some fruit.

BIG QUESTION 4

When do we use subtraction?

B **Complete the sentences. Use the past tense.**

1 Joe's mother ___had___ ten cookies. Joe ___ate___ five cookies. (have, eat)

2 The baker _____ twelve apple pies. He _____ three. (make, sell)

3 Thirteen monkeys _____ in a tree. Nine _____ away. (hide, run)

4 Bobby _____ six birds. Two _____ away. (buy, fly)

C **Write the questions. Then answer them.**

1 ten / buy / did / Anna / pencils ?
 Did Anna buy ten pencils?
 Yes, she did.

2 cook / did / soup / the / make ?

3 eat / pies / you / how many / did ?

4 did / what / drink / Andy ?

Review 73

UNIT 9 Get Ready

BIG QUESTION 5

How do people get along with each other?

Think about the Big Question. Write.

What do you know?

_____
_____
_____
_____
_____
_____
_____

What do you want to know?

_____
_____
_____
_____
_____
_____
_____

Words

A Look at the pictures and write the words.

take turns	litter	lifeguard
polite	clean up	librarian

1. _take turns_

2. _____

3. _____

4. _____

5. _____

6. _____

74 Unit 9   Vocabulary: Rules and People   Student Book page 88

B Complete the chart.

> ~~librarian~~   take turns   clean up   litter
> crossing guard   principal   lifeguard

People	Actions
1 __librarian__	5 _____
2 _____	6 _____
3 _____	7 _____
4 _____	

C Circle *True* or *False*.

1 Crossing guards and traffic lights help keep us safe.   (True)   False
2 It's polite to take turns with friends.   True   False
3 It's good to litter.   True   False
4 We should always clean up after we play.   True   False
5 Lifeguards keep us safe at the beach.   True   False
6 Principals don't make the school rules.   True   False

D Change the underlined words to make the sentences correct.

1 The <u>crossing guard</u> helps us find books in the library. __librarian__
2 The children <u>litter</u> after they bake cookies. _____
3 The <u>principal</u> works at a swimming pool and keeps us safe there. _____
4 The <u>librarian</u> keeps children safe on the street. _____
5 Jimmy and Susie don't fight on the playground because they <u>clean up</u> on the swing. _____
6 The street is dirty. Students shouldn't <u>take turns in</u> the street. _____
7 The <u>lifeguard</u> helps all the students and teachers in a school. _____

Read

A Read the text quickly. Answer the question.

In a museum, who can we ask for help?

___

A VISIT TO A Museum

A museum is a great place where we can look at lots of interesting things. You can learn a lot and have fun, too. There are rules we should follow in a museum so everyone can enjoy their visit.

These are some of those rules:
- Be quiet. Don't shout or be too loud.
- Be thoughtful. Take turns so everyone can look at the things.
- Be safe. Don't run in the museum and don't jump on things.
- Ask a guard when you need help.
- Don't touch things that aren't yours.
- Listen to your teacher.
- Keep the museum clean. Don't litter.
- Eat and drink only in the museum cafeteria.
- Clean up after you eat.

Think

What should you do in a museum?
What shouldn't you do in a museum?

Understand

Comprehension

A What part of the text do you like? Check (✓).

The things you can see ☐   The things you should do ☐
The things you shouldn't do ☐

B What should and shouldn't you do in a museum? Write four things each.

Things We Should Do	Things We Shouldn't Do
1 ____be quiet____	5 _____
2 _____	6 _____
3 _____	7 _____
4 _____	8 _____

C Circle the correct words.

1 I walk in the museum. I ask a guard for help. I want to be **(safe)** / **clean**.

2 I look at something, then I move, and then my friend looks at it. I want to be **quiet** / **thoughtful**.

3 My teacher says, "Sit down," and I sit down. I want to be **good** / **clean**.

4 I'm hungry. I ask my teacher, "Where can I put my plastic lunch bag?" I want to keep the museum **dirty** / **clean**.

5 I look at all the interesting things. I don't touch them. I want to be **dirty** / **good**.

6 I am excited, but I don't shout. I want to be **quiet** / **clean**.

7 My friend calls me. I don't run. I want to be **safe** / **dirty**.

8 My teacher talks. I listen. I want to be **good** / **safe**.

Comprehension   Unit 9   77

Grammar in Use

A Study the grammar.

Learn Possessive Pronouns

| This | is / isn't | my / your / his / her / its / our / their | ball. |

| This ball | is / isn't | mine. / yours. / his. / hers. / ours. / theirs. |

| Is this ball | yours? / his? / hers? / theirs? |

| Yes, | it | is. |
| No, | it | isn't. |

| Whose ball is this? |

| It's | mine. / yours. / his. / hers. / ours. / theirs. |

B Complete the chart

I	my	mine
	your	
		his
she		
		its
	our	
they		

C Circle the correct word.

1. That book has her name on it. It's **his** / **(hers)**.
2. This jacket is **his** / **mine**. My grandmother gave it to me.
3. Those cookies are **ours** / **theirs**. They baked them yesterday.
4. He's a librarian. This desk is **his** / **hers**.
5. Are these sneakers **its** / **yours**?
6. That treehouse is **theirs** / **ours**. We built it together.

D Look at the pictures and answer the questions.

1. Whose kitten is that?
   It's hers.

2. Whose notebooks are those?
   _____

3. Whose doll is that?
   _____

4. Whose cap is this?
   _____

5. Whose cake is this?
   _____

Grammar: Possessive Pronouns   Unit 9   79

Communicate

Words

A Look and number the pictures.

1. crosswalk
2. classroom
3. swimming pool
4. kitchen
5. living room
6. cafeteria

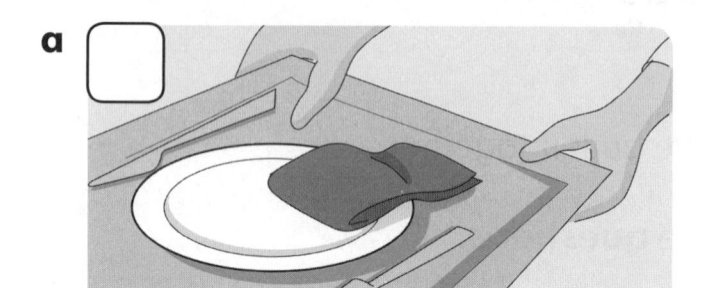

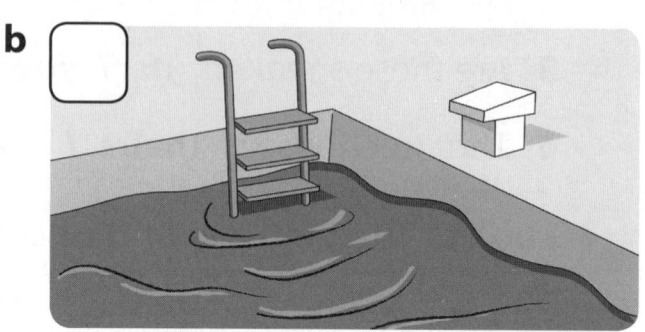

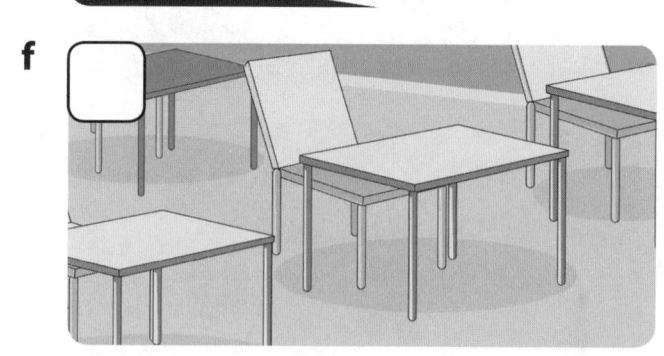

a.
b.
c.
d. 1
e.
f.

B Read the words and write the places.

1. swim   water   lifeguard: _____ swimming pool _____
2. couch   lamp   watch TV: _____
3. street traffic lights crossing guard: _____
4. school food   eat lunch: _____
5. chairs teacher   desks: _____
6. food   cook   home: _____

80 Unit 9 *Vocabulary*   Student Book page 94

Word Study

A Circle the correct word.

1. take **up** / **away**
2. stand **down** / **up**
3. clean **up** / **away**
4. fall **down** / **away**

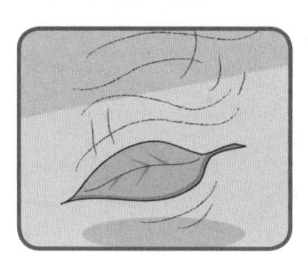

Writing

A Read about the rules at Kate's house.

> My mother makes the rules at my house for my brother and me. We should clean our rooms every day. We should do our homework before we watch TV. We shouldn't go to bed late.

B Complete the chart about the rules at your house.

Who makes the rules?	
Rule 1	
Rule 2	
Rule 3	

C Now write about the rules at your house.

_____
_____
_____
_____

Writing: Phrasal Verbs **Unit 9** **81**

UNIT 10 Get Ready

Words

A Look at the picture. Number the words.

_6_ wash	___ knock	___ put away
___ grab	___ pass	___ share

82 Unit 10 Vocabulary: Getting Along

Student Book page 96

B Complete the puzzle. Then find the secret word and complete the sentence.

	1 p	a	s	s	
2					
3					
		4			
5					

Remember! It's good to _____ things with your friends!

C Circle the correct word.

1 It's very _____ to grab food at the table.
  a nice   b (rude)

2 It's good to _____ your toys with your friends.
  a share   b wash

3 It's _____ to take turns when we play on the swings.
  a nice   b rude

4 You should always _____ your hands before you eat.
  a put away   b wash

Vocabulary: Getting Along   Unit 10   83

Read

A Read the story quickly. Answer the question.

Who shared all the food at lunch?
_____

Lunch at Frog's House

Frog invited Turtle and Lizard for lunch. Turtle knocked on the door and asked, "May I come in?" Lizard didn't knock or ask. He just opened the door and walked in. Turtle brought fruit for Frog. Lizard didn't bring anything. Turtle washed before he came to the table, but Lizard didn't.

Think Is Turtle polite?

At lunch Turtle shared all the food. Lizard grabbed all the fruit and didn't share it. Turtle asked Frog to pass the food, but Lizard just grabbed his.

After lunch, Turtle helped Frog clean up, but Lizard went home early. He didn't say, "Thank you." or "Goodbye."

Think Is Lizard thoughtful?

Turtle invited Frog for lunch the next day, but he didn't invite Lizard. Do you know why?

Understand

Comprehension

A What part of the story do you like? Check (✓).

Frog ☐   Turtle ☐   Lizard ☐

B Circle the correct the theme of the story.

1 It's fun to have lunch with friends.

2 We should eat a lot of fruit.

3 We should always be polite and thoughtful.

C Circle *True* or *False*. Correct the false statements.

1 Turtle invited Frog and Lizard to lunch.

True   (False)   Frog invited Turtle and Lizard.

2 Lizard is polite.

True   False   _____

3 Lizard brought food to share.

True   False   _____

4 Turtle is thoughtful.

True   False   _____

5 Turtle cleaned up after lunch.

True   False   _____

6 Lizard left before Turtle.

True   False   _____

7 Turtle, Frog, and Lizard have lunch together the next day.

True   False   _____

Grammar in Use

A Study the grammar.

Learn Can and May

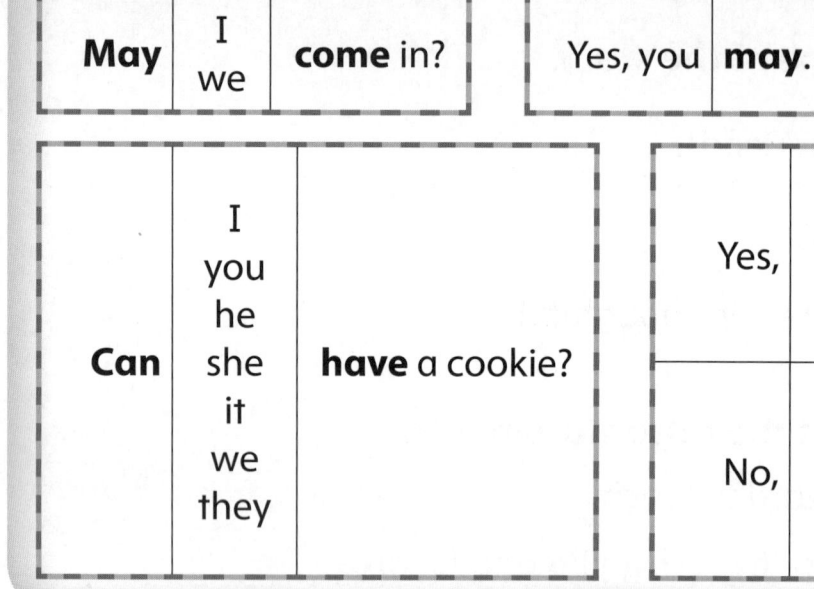

| **May** | I / we | **come** in? |

Yes, you **may**.

No, you **may not**.

| **Can** | I / you / he / she / it / we / they | **have** a cookie? |

Yes, I / you / he — **can**.
No, she / it / we / they — **can't**.

B Match the beginnings of the sentences to the ends.

1. Can I have
2. May we come
3. May I use
4. Can he bring
5. May we play
6. Can she come
7. Can they show
8. May I open

a a game on the Internet?
b in?
c with us?
d some apple juice?
e your phone?
f the window?
g his dog?
h you their art project?

C Look at the pictures. Write the questions and complete the answers.

1

Can / watch TV?

 Can we watch TV?

No, you can't.

2

May / use your ruler?

_____

Yes, _____

3

Can / have a sandwich?

_____

Yes, _____

4

May / go outside?

_____

No, _____

5

Can / play a video game?

_____

No, _____

6

May / go to the playground?

_____

Yes, _____

D Check (✓) the questions you ask at home.

1 ☐ May I watch TV?

2 ☐ Can I play outside?

3 ☐ May I go on the Internet?

4 ☐ Can I make a sandwich?

5 ☐ May I have some soda?

6 ☐ Can I play a video game?

Grammar: Using Can *and* May   **Unit 10**   **87**

Communicate

Words

A Circle the correct word.

1. (computer) / headphones
2. laptop / camera
3. tablet / cell phone
4. tablet / headphones
5. computer / cell phone
6. laptop / camera

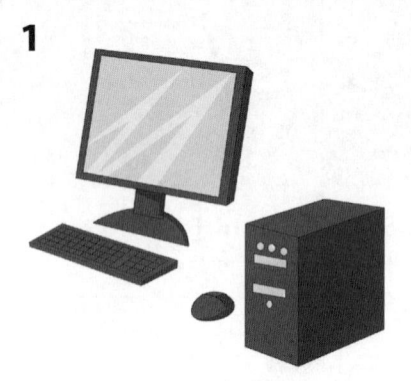

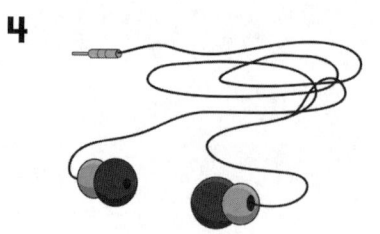

B Complete the chart with the words in **A**.

We Can Play Games On It	We Can't Play Games On It
1. computer	5. _____
2. _____	6. _____
3. _____	
4. _____	

88 Unit 10 *Vocabulary: Technology* Student Book page 102

Writing Study

A Complete the sentences.

1. It __was__ clean yesterday. It __is__ dirty now.
2. I _____ happy yesterday. I _____ sad today.
3. Her students _____ rude yesterday. They _____ polite today.
4. My parents _____ in Italy yesterday. They _____ in England today.
5. It _____ sunny yesterday. It _____ raining now.
6. The dog _____ quiet yesterday. It _____ loud today.

Writing

A Read about Janet, a very thoughtful person.

> Janet is my friend. She's a very thoughtful person. She takes turns. She always shares her candy, too. She puts away her toys and cleans up. She is never loud, and she never grabs things.

B Think about a rude or a thoughtful person. Answer the questions.

1. What's the person's name? _____
2. Is he / she thoughtful or rude? _____
3. What does he / she always do? _____
4. What does he / she never do? _____

C Now write about that person.

_____
_____
_____
_____
_____
_____

What have you learned?

Review

A Write the words and match the words to the pictures.

1. haws
   wash — b

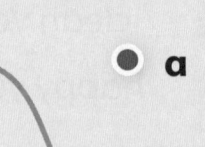

2. cfirtaf ghilt —

3. nkokc —

4. lcle epnho —

a, b,  c,  d

B Match the beginnings of the sentences to the ends.

1. "May I have — d an apple?" "Yes, you may."

2. "Whose cookies — a to the park?" "Yes, you can."

3. "Are those — b pens theirs?" "No, they're his."

4. "Can we walk — c computer hers?" "Yes, it is."

5. "Whose cell phone — e is this?" "It's his."

6. "Is this — f are these?" "They're mine."

BIG QUESTION 5

How do people get along with each other?

90

C Look at the pictures. Complete the questions and write the answers.

1 Can we go _____ ?
_____

2 Whose _____ ?
_____

3 May I use _____ ?
_____

4 Is this _____ ?
_____

D Complete the sentences.

down   are   ~~up~~   were   away   was

1 We're cleaning ____up____ the classroom.
2 Miguel and Tim _____ in the living room now.
3 My mother put _____ the cookies after lunch.
4 I _____ very tired yesterday.
5 The students always sit _____ on the school bus.
6 My friends and I _____ at the swimming pool yesterday.

Review   91

UNIT 11 Get Ready

BIG QUESTION 6

Why should we take care of the Earth?

Think about the Big Question. Write.

What do you know?

_____
_____
_____
_____
_____
_____
_____

What do you want to know?

_____
_____
_____
_____
_____
_____
_____

Words

A Circle the correct word for each picture.

1. **resources** / sunlight

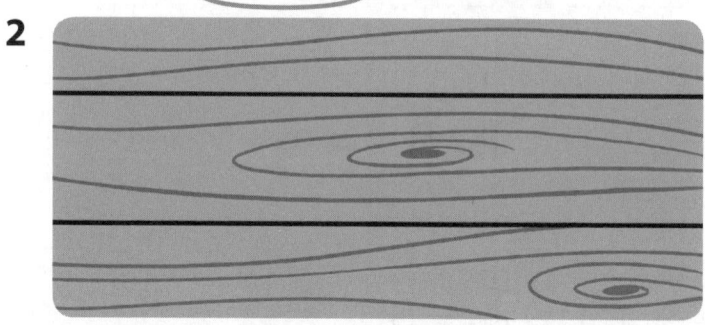

2. trash / **wood**

3. land / **landfill**

4. **trash** / smoke

92   Unit 11   Vocabulary: Land and Resources   Student Book page 109

B Complete the chart.

> ~~water~~   land   trash   smoke   sunlight
> wood   landfill

Natural Resources	Hurting Natural Resources
1 _____water_____	5 _____
2 _____	6 _____
3 _____	7 _____
4 _____	

C Match the beginnings of the sentences to the ends.

1 It isn't thoughtful to
2 On a sunny day, there's
3 There's a lot of trash
4 I wash a jar and put things in it,
5 We should take care of

a in landfills.
b so I reuse it.
c throw trash on the ground.
d the earth's resources.
e a lot of sunlight.

(1 matches with c)

D Circle the incorrect words. Write the correct words.

1 I reuse plastic bags. I want to (throw) the trash I make. _____reduce_____

2 The farmer plants vegetables on his landfill. _____

3 It isn't healthy to breathe air with steam in it. _____

4 We get pasta from trees. _____

5 Water, trees, air, and land are landfills. _____

6 Smoke and trash are good for the natural resources. _____

Vocabulary: Land and Resources Words   Unit 11

Read

A **Read the text quickly. Answer the question.**
Where does most of the water we drink come from?

Water

Water is a very important natural resource, and we need to take care of it. People, animals, plants, and trees all need water to live and grow. We also need water to keep us clean and healthy and to wash our things.

To get clean rainwater we need clean air. Most of the water we drink comes from rain. There are drops of rain in clouds above us. When rain falls through dirty air, it gets dirty. When rain falls through clean air, it doesn't get dirty.

Think
What's the main idea?
What is a detail?

Sometimes people don't take care of water. They use too much water or throw trash in it and make it dirty. Sometimes oil goes into the sea from big ships, and this makes the water dirty. Dirty water isn't healthy for people, fish, birds, and other animals.

Think
What's the main idea?
What is a detail?

We all need to take care of water, because all living things need it.

Understand

Comprehension

A What part of the text do you like? Check (✓).

The animals ☐   The water ☐   The clean air ☐

B Answer the questions.

Paragraph 1

1 What is the main idea?
_____

2 What is one detail?
_____

C Circle *True* or *False*. For false statements, circle the incorrect word, then write the correct word.

1 Water is important because (nonliving) things need it to live and grow.

   True   (False)   ____living____

2 A lot of the water we drink comes from the ground.

   True   False   _____

3 Dirty air means dirty water.

   True   False   _____

4 Trash is good for fish.

   True   False   _____

5 Fish put oil in the water. This makes the water dangerous.

   True   False   _____

6 People should use a lot of water every day.

   True   False   _____

7 When people and animals drink dirty water, they can get sick.

   True   False   _____

Comprehension   Unit 11   95

Grammar in Use

A Study the grammar.

Learn Prepositions of Place

| The honeybee is | above
across from
behind
in front of
between | the flowers. |

B Look at the pictures and circle the correct words.

1. The plants are **behind** / **(between)** the flowers.

2. The lake is **above** / **in front of** the woods.

3. The bird is **above** / **across** from the building.

4. The school is **across from** / **behind** the park.

5. The squirrels are **between** / **behind** the tree.

6. The rabbit is **above** / **between** the cats.

96 Unit 11 *Grammar: Prepositions of Place* Student Book page 113

C Look at the pictures and complete the sentences.

1. The roses are ___between___ the statues.

2. The smoke is _____ the factory.

3. The bench is _____ the fountain.

4. The fish is _____ the seaweed.

5. The table is _____ the chairs.

6. The TV is _____ the couch.

D Answer the questions about your bedroom.

1. Where is your bed? _____
2. Where is your chair? _____
3. Where is the window? _____
4. Where is the door? _____
5. Where are your books? _____
6. Where are your shoes? _____

Communicate

Words

A Look and number the pictures.

> **1** camp **2** hike **3** fish **4** surf **5** ski **6** horse ride

a. 3

b.

c.

d.

e.

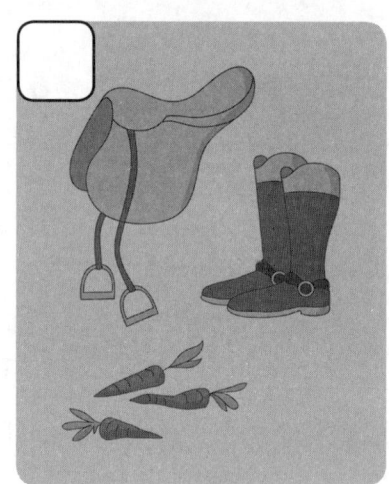

f.

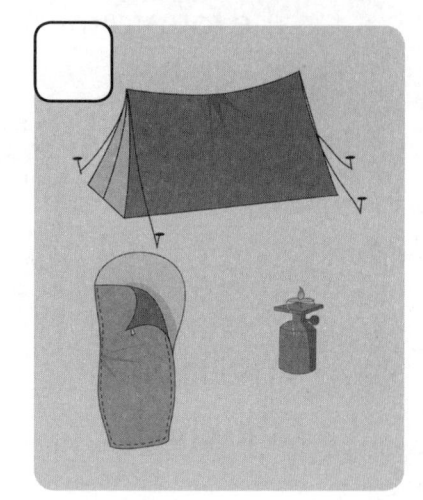

B Complete the chart with the words from **A**.

Things People Do In the Ocean	Things People Don't Do In the Ocean
1 _____fish_____	3 _____
2 _____	4 _____
	5 _____
	6 _____

98 Unit 11 *Vocabulary: Sports*

Word Study

A Complete the chart.

~~sunlight~~ reuse us yours rude wood
dirty theirs tired share city make

Verbs	Nouns	Adjectives	Pronouns
1 _____	4 sunlight	7 _____	10 _____
2 _____	5 _____	8 _____	11 _____
3 _____	6 _____	9 _____	12 _____

B Circle the verbs in blue, the nouns in red, the adjectives in black, and the pronouns in green.

1 The greedy dog ate my sandwich.
2 Eddie gave me a red pencil.
3 We used the old computer.
4 I played with them at the big park.

Writing

A Read about the natural resources Kareem sees every day.

> I see water when I wash my hands. I see trees when I use paper. I see sunlight when it's sunny outside.

B Write three natural resources you see every day.

1 _____ 2 _____ 3 _____

C Now write about them.

_____
_____
_____

UNIT 12 Get Ready

Words

A Circle the odd one out.

1	stationery store:	paper	diary	(carton)
2	recycling plant:	land	machine	paper
3	shelf:	landfill	museum	stationery store
4	rescue:	people	trash	animals
5	recycle:	paper	landfill	carton
6	place:	recycling plant	museum	trash

B Write words from **A** under the correct picture.

1. carton
2. 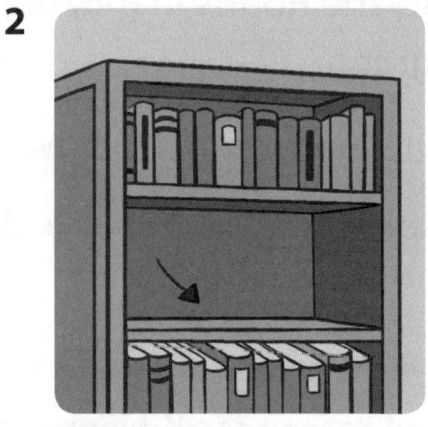 
3. 
4. 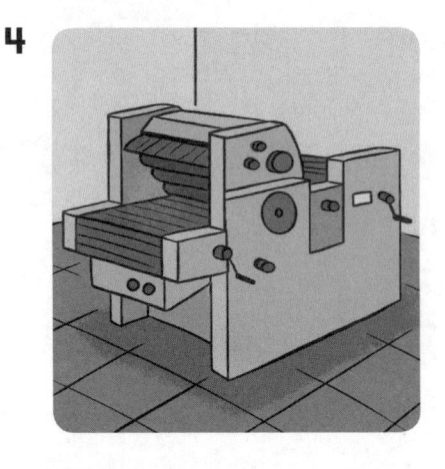
5. 
6.

100 Unit 12 *Vocabulary: Recycling* Student Book page 116

C Circle *True* or *False*.

1. A recycling plant makes new things from old things. **(True)** **False**
2. Machines help people make things. **True** **False**
3. Sunlight can blow a kite into a tree. **True** **False**
4. People who rescue animals are very fierce. **True** **False**
5. A carton is a container and often has juice in it. **True** **False**
6. We write on paper. We can buy paper in many colors. **True** **False**

D Read and write the words. Find the mystery word and answer the question.

1. This place sells paper and pencils.
   s t a t i o n e r y s t o r e
2. This place helps us reuse paper, glass, and plastic things.
   _ _ _ _ _ _ _ _ _ _ _ _ _ _
3. We write things on this.
   _ _ _ _ _
4. We put things like books on this.
   _ _ _ _ _
5. We can see this in a factory. It can be noisy.
   _ _ _ _ _ _ _

What is something you should never throw on the ground? _____

Read

A **Read the story quickly. Answer the question.**
The people near Turtle are doing something they shouldn't do. What is it?

___

Turtle's Diary

June 15
Dear Diary,
I'm swimming in the lake. There are some fish below me and above me. My turtle friends are sitting on stones in the sun. There are people having a picnic near the lake. Oh, no, they're littering!

Think
Where is the turtle?

June 16
Dear Diary,
I'm in the lake again today. What's that I see below me? Fish? No. I see cartons and plastic bags. It's trash from the picnic! Oh, no! A plastic bag is around my leg. It's hard to swim, so I climb up on a rock.

June 17
Dear Diary,
This plastic bag is still on my leg. I'm sad because I can't go in the water. Look! It's a man in a boat. He rescues me. Please don't litter! It's bad for all living things.

Understand

Comprehension

A What part of the story do you like? Check (✓).

The turtles ☐   The plastic bag ☐   The man in the boat ☐

B Circle the correct setting of the story.

1 the ocean   2 a pond   3 a lake

C Circle the correct answers.

1 Turtle is swimming. He's _____ .
   a fierce   b tired   c (happy)

2 There are some _____ in the water.
   a birds   b fish   c stones

3 There are turtles on _____ .
   a the water   b the sun   c stones

4 Turtle sees people throwing trash on the ground. He's _____ .
   a calm   b angry   c hungry

5 Trash from the picnic goes into _____ .
   a the stones   b the water   c the picnic

6 A _____ is around Turtle's leg.
   a carton   b plastic bag   c plastic bottle

7 Turtle is on the rock. He _____ in the water.
   a wants to go   b doesn't want to go   c goes

8 Turtle says littering is bad for _____ .
   a people   b animals   c people, animals, and plants

Comprehension Unit 12 103

Grammar in Use

A Study the grammar.

Learn Prepositions of Place

Is / Was	there	a carton	behind the trash can?
Are / Were		cartons	

Where	is / was	the carton?
	are / were	the cartons?

Yes,	there	is / was.
		are / were.
No,		isn't / wasn't.
		aren't / weren't.

It	is / was	behind the trash can.
They	are / were	

B Circle the correct words.

1 **Is** / Are there a statue in the park? Yes / **No**, there **isn't** / aren't.

2 Were / **Where** are the trash cans? It's / **They're** across from the trees.

3 Where is / **are** the boys? It's / **They're** in front of the school.

4 Is / **Are** there smoke above the car? Yes / **No**, there **isn't** / aren't.

5 **Was** / Were there a store behind the school? Yes / **No**, there **was** / were.

C Answer the questions.

1 Was there a lake behind the trees? ✓ <u>Yes, there was.</u>

2 Are there children in the playground? ✗ _____

3 Is there smoke above the recycle plant? ✗ _____

4 Were there plants in front of the school? ✓ _____

5 Were there many swimmers in the pool? ✓ _____

6 Is there a book on the table? ✗ _____

7 Was there a lifeguard at the beach? ✓ _____

8 Are there many trees in the park? ✓ _____

D Look at the pictures and answer the questions.

1. Was the pond behind the woods?
No, it wasn't.

2. Where is the stationery store?
_____

3. Are there shelves above the desk?
_____

4. Were the fish in the lake?
_____

5. Is the statue in front of the window?
_____

6. Where is the school?
_____

E Answer the questions.

1 Where is your backpack? _____
2 Is there a clock above your desk? _____
3 Where is your trash can? _____
4 Is there a park across from your house? _____

Grammar: Prepositions of Place with Wh- and Yes/No Questions **Unit 12** **105**

Communicate

Words

A Look at the chart. Circle the correct words.

	Picked Up Trash At School	Visited a Recycling Plant	Walked To the Park	Planted Flowers
June's Class	9:15	11:00	2:00	2:15
Ali's Class	2:30	8:45	11:15	11:30
Nadia's Class	11:45	9:30	12:45	1:00

1 All the classes did the same things at different **(times)** / **weeks**.

2 June's class walked to the park at **twelve o'clock** / **two o'clock**.

3 June's class visited a recycling plant at **eleven o'clock** / **eight o'clock**.

4 Ali's class planted flowers at **five-fifteen** / **eleven-thirty**.

5 Ali's class picked up trash at school at **two-thirty** / **twelve-thirty**.

6 Nadia's class planted flowers at **eleven o'clock** / **one o'clock**.

B Look at the chart in **A** and answer the questions.

1 What time did Nadia's class visit a recycling plant?
   They visited a recycling plant at nine-thirty.

2 What time did June's class pick up trash at school?
   _____

3 What time did Ali's class walk to the park?
   _____

4 Did Nadia's class walk to the park at two forty-five?
   _____

5 Did June's class plant flowers at eleven-thirty?
   _____

6 Did Ali's class visit a recycling plant at eight o'clock?
   _____

106 Unit 12 *Vocabulary: Time*

Writing Study

A Circle the correct words.

1 Mohamed **cleans** / **is cleaning** / **(cleaned)** his room yesterday.

2 My sisters **recycle** / **are recycling** / **recycled** their juice cartons every day.

3 I **rescue** / **am rescuing** / **rescued** the cat from a tree yesterday.

4 The wind **blows** / **is blowing** / **blew** the leaves off the trees now.

5 I **walk** / **am walking** / **walked** to school and I'm late.

6 The boys **play** / **are playing** / **played** football yesterday.

Writing

A Read. Wendy imagined she was a recycled newspaper.

> I was an old newspaper. A thoughtful girl put me in the recycle bin. I went to the recycling plant. Now I am a new paper bag!

B Imagine you are something that was a recycled thing. Answer the questions.

1 What were you? _____

2 How did you get to the recycling bin? _____

3 Where did you go? _____

4 What are you now? _____

C Now write the story.

_____
_____
_____
_____
_____

What have you learned?

_____
_____
_____
_____
_____
_____
_____
_____
_____
_____
_____
_____
_____
_____
_____
_____
_____

BIG QUESTION 6

Why should we take care of the Earth?

108

Review

A Write *T* (*True*) or *F* (*False*). Correct the false statements.

1. It's three-thirty. __F__
   It's three forty-five.

2. This is a landfill. ____
   _____

3. I'm in a stationery store. ____
   _____

4. This is a week. ____
   _____

5. These are resources. ____
   _____

B Write the sentences.

1 across from / The park / the stationery store / is
   The park is across from the stationery store.

2 the couch / The clock / was / above
   _____

3 Joey and Frank / between / The teacher / is
   _____

4 the benches / in front of / The roses / were
   _____

C Match the questions to the answers.

1 Where's the landfill?
2 Where were the cartons?
3 Were the toys behind the couch?
4 Are the buses in front of the school?

a Yes, they are.
b No, they weren't.
c It's behind the recycling plant.
d They were in the recycling plant.

D Look at the pictures and write where Turtle is.

1 Turtle is above the carton.

2 _____

3 _____

4 _____

Review **109**

BIG QUESTION 7

How does music make us feel?

Think about the Big Question. Write.

What do you know?
_____
_____
_____
_____
_____
_____
_____

What do you want to know?
_____
_____
_____
_____
_____
_____
_____

UNIT 13 Get Ready

Words

A Look at the pictures and circle the correct word.

1. tambourine / (trumpet)

2. sleepy / excited

3. right / wrong

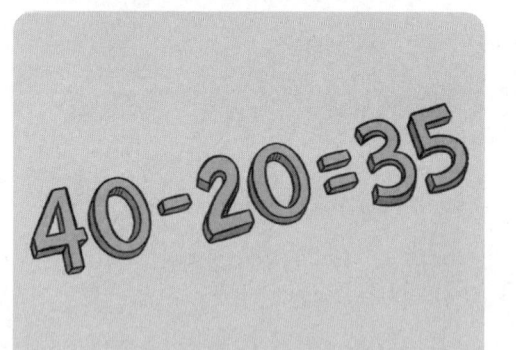

4. high / low

110 Unit 13   Vocabulary: Music • Feelings   Student Book page 128

B Look at the code. Write the words, then match the words to the pictures.

1	2	3	4	5	6	7	8	9	10	11	12	13	14
a	b	c	d	e	f	g	h	i	j	k	l	m	n

15	16	17	18	19	20	21	22	23	24	25	26
o	p	q	r	s	t	u	v	w	x	y	z

a 6 5 5 12 9 14 7 19 __feelings__

b 23 15 12 6 _____

c 5 24 3 9 20 5 4 _____

d 12 15 23 _____

e 19 12 5 5 16 25 _____

C Circle *True or False.*

1 A wolf can be a pet.   True   (False)
2 A mobile phone can be sleepy.   True   False
3 We blow a trumpet to play it.   True   False
4 A trumpet can play loud and soft music.   True   False

D Change the underlined words to make the sentences true.

1 It's 2 o'clock in the morning. She's very <u>wrong</u>. s<u>leepy</u>
2 He played a high note on his <u>tambourine</u>. t_____
3 I have a new computer. I'm very <u>sleepy</u>. e_____
4 Four plus four equals nine is the <u>right</u> answer. w_____

Read

A **Read the text quickly. Answer the question.**

What's the opposite of loud music?

_____

Music is all around us

A lot of people listen to music when they go places or do things. Some people listen to music when they jog or run in the morning. Some people listen to music when they're in the car so they don't feel sleepy. Many people listen to music when they read books or study. Do you listen to music when you study?

Think
What's the most important part?

People often listen to music with others. They go to concerts or to parties, or they play music when they get together with friends and family. Some people sing along with the music, and other people dance to the music. Music helps us have a happy time.

Think
What's the most important part?

There are many different types of music. Some people like one type of music, and some people like many different types of music. Sometimes the music is very loud, and sometimes it's soft. Does loud music make you feel excited? Does soft music make you feel calm?

Think
What's the most important part?

We can hear music in lots of places. The next time you go out, listen. Do you hear music? How does it make you feel?

Understand

Comprehension

A What part of the text do you like? Check (✓).

Listening to music ☐   Loud music ☐   Soft music ☐

B Think of the most important parts of the text. Summarize the text.

People listen to music when they go places or do things.

C Read the text again and answer the questions.

1 What do some people do in the morning?

2 Why do some people listen to music in the car?

3 Where do people share music? Write three situations.

  a
  b
  c

4 What do people do when they listen to music? Write two things.

  a
  b

5 How do people feel when they listen to music? Write two things.

  a
  b

6 Is music important to a lot of people? Why/Why not?

Comprehension   Unit 13   113

Grammar in Use

A Study the grammar.

Learn Prepositions of Time

| When | do you listen to music? |
| What time | |

I listen to music	in the	morning. afternoon. evening.
	at	night. 4:00.
	on	Sunday.

B Read and circle the correct word.
1. My grandmother listens to music in the **night** / **morning**.
2. Michelle and I practice the piano at **afternoon** / **two-thirty**.
3. They usually watch TV in the **evening** / **night**.
4. My sister and I jog on **Saturday** / **morning**.
5. Jennifer goes to dance class at **Tuesday** / **four fifteen**.
6. Rick and his brother stay up late on **night** / **Saturday**.

C Complete the sentences with *in the*, *at*, or *on*.
1. My brother and I have lunch with our grandparents ___on___ Sunday.
2. Helen has a piano lesson _____ five o'clock.
3. The students clean up the classroom _____ afternoon.
4. Do Liz and Benny play video games _____ night? No, they don't.
5. Does your cat come home _____ evening? Yes, he does.
6. Mark doesn't practice the flute _____ morning.

114 Unit 13 *Grammar: Prepositional Phrases of Time with* in, on, at

Student Book page 133

D Look at the pictures and answer the questions.

1 When does Nancy watch TV?
   In the evening.

2 What time does Sally get up?
   _____

3 What time does Jim go to bed?
   _____

4 What time does Lucy eat lunch?
   _____

5 When does Tommy run?
   _____

6 When does Amy go to art class?
   _____

E Answer the questions.

1 Do you listen to music in the morning?
   _____

2 Do you go to school at eight o'clock?
   _____

3 Do you watch TV in the evening?
   _____

Grammar: Prepositional Phrases of Time with in, on, at   **Unit 13**   **115**

Communicate

Words

A Look at the pictures and number the words.

1  2  3

4  5  6

___ proud	___ crying	___ unhappy
___ yawning	___ smiling	_1_ nervous

B Circle the correct word.

1 Mike can't go to the park with his friends.
   He's crying. He's **proud / unhappy**.

2 Linda is singing in the front of the class.
   Her hands are shaking. She's **nervous / yawning**.

3 Paul's test score is 100. He's smiling. He's **nervous / proud**.

4 It's late and Jose is tired. He's **yawning / proud**.

5 Nadia has a new computer. She's happy. She's **crying / smiling**.

116   Unit 13   Vocabulary: Action • Feelings   Student Book page 134

Word Study

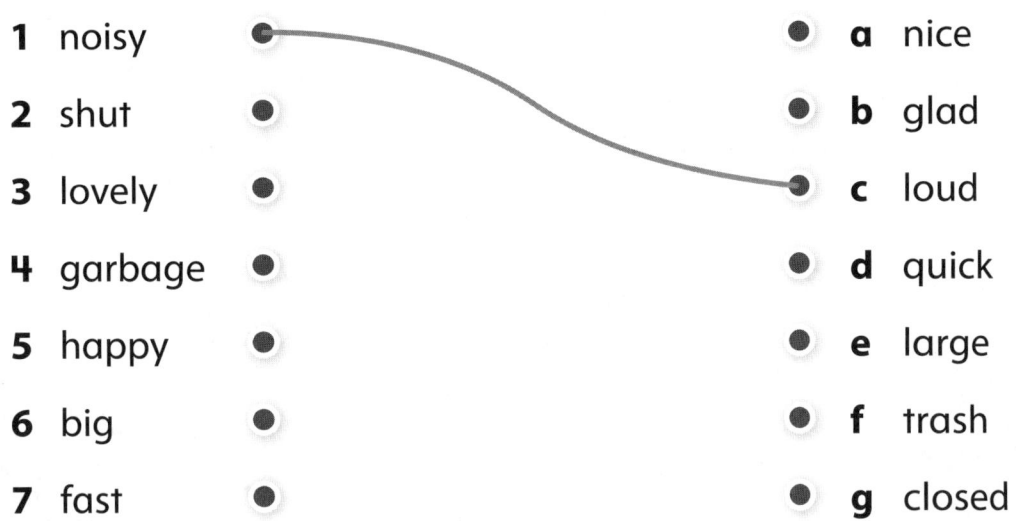

A Match the words to a synonym.

1 noisy — c loud
2 shut
3 lovely
4 garbage
5 happy
6 big
7 fast

a nice
b glad
c loud
d quick
e large
f trash
g closed

Writing

A Read about how music made Jody feel.

> It was morning. I was in my room, and I was very sleepy. I listened to some fast piano music. It was fun. It made me feel excited.

B Think about a time you listened to music. Answer the questions.

1 When was it? _____
2 Where were you? _____
3 What music did you listen to? _____
4 How did it make you feel? _____

C Now write about how the music made you feel.

_____
_____
_____
_____

Writing: Synonyms Unit 13 117

UNIT 14 Get Ready

Words

A Look at the pictures and write the letters.

- **a** record
- **b** worried
- **c** hummingbird
- **d** notes
- **e** musician
- **f** the flu
- **g** tears
- **h** wait
- **i** solo

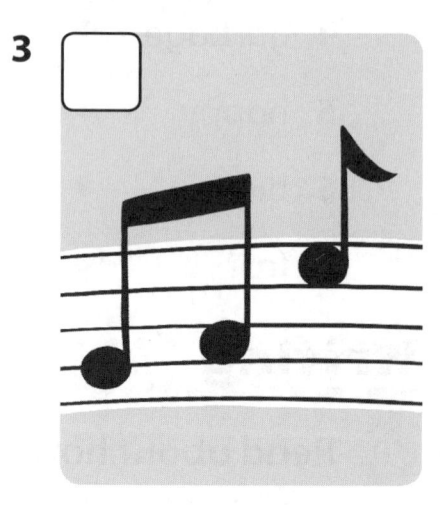

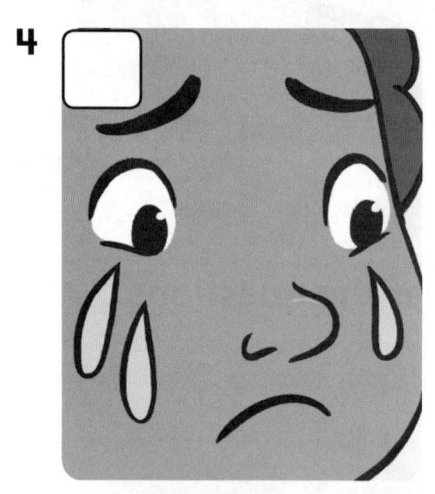

1. i
2.
3.
4.
5.
6.
7.
8.
9.

118 Unit 14 Vocabulary: Music • Feelings Student Book page 136

B Match the beginnings to the ends of the sentences.

1 He's tired because
2 He has tears in his eyes because
3 He's smiling because
4 He's running because
5 He plays the drums every day because
6 He didn't study. He's worried because

a he's very late for school.
b he's a musician in a band.
c he feels sad and tired.
d he has a math test today.
e he didn't sleep well yesterday.
f he passed his math test yesterday.

(1 matches to e)

C Write the words.

a umhnmgiibdr _____hummingbird_____
b onets _____
c aetsr _____
d oerdwir _____
e umaiinsc _____
f sloo _____

D Complete the sentences.

1 That _____hummingbird_____ is pretty and very small.
2 My brother plays the trumpet in a band. He's a _____.
3 That song has a very good guitar _____.
4 My sister is _____ because she didn't study.
5 She can play high and low _____ on her trumpet.
6 On very cold days we sometimes get _____ in our eyes.

Vocabulary: Music • Feelings   Unit 14   119

Read

A Read the story quickly. Answer the question.

Who listened to music on the school bus?

Sarah Loves Music

Sarah loves music. It helps her feel happy when she feels bad, and calm when she's nervous.

> **Think**
> What character is in this part?

Last week, Sarah had a fight with her best friend at school. She felt very sad, so she listened to some happy music after school. Then she felt good.

> **Think**
> What character is in this part?

This morning, Sarah had a math test. She doesn't like math because she thinks it's boring. She listened to some fast music. She felt happy when she took the test. Her test score was 95! She was very proud.

Yesterday, Sarah was worried because she had an important soccer game in the afternoon. So she listened to some slow music before the game. She felt calm, and they won the game! What do you think? Did the music help them win?

On the way home Sarah and her soccer friends listened to pop music on the school bus. They sang their favorite songs and had a good time!

> **Think**
> What character is in this part?

Music is an important part of Sarah's day.

Understand

Comprehension

A What part of the story do you like? Check (✓).

Fast music ☐   Slow music ☐   Pop music ☐

B Answer the questions.

1. Who is the main character? _____
2. Who are the secondary characters? _____

C Complete the chart.

Sarah had …	Sarah felt …	Sarah listened to …	Sarah felt …
1 a fight with her best friend.	_____.	happy music.	_____.
2 _____.	bored.	_____.	_____.
3 _____.	worried.	_____.	_____.

D Answer the questions.

1. Does music change Sarah's feelings? <u>Yes it does.</u>
2. Did Sarah do well on her math test? _____
3. Is Sarah lonely? _____
4. Does Sarah like to sing? _____
5. Does Sarah often listen to music? _____

Grammar in Use

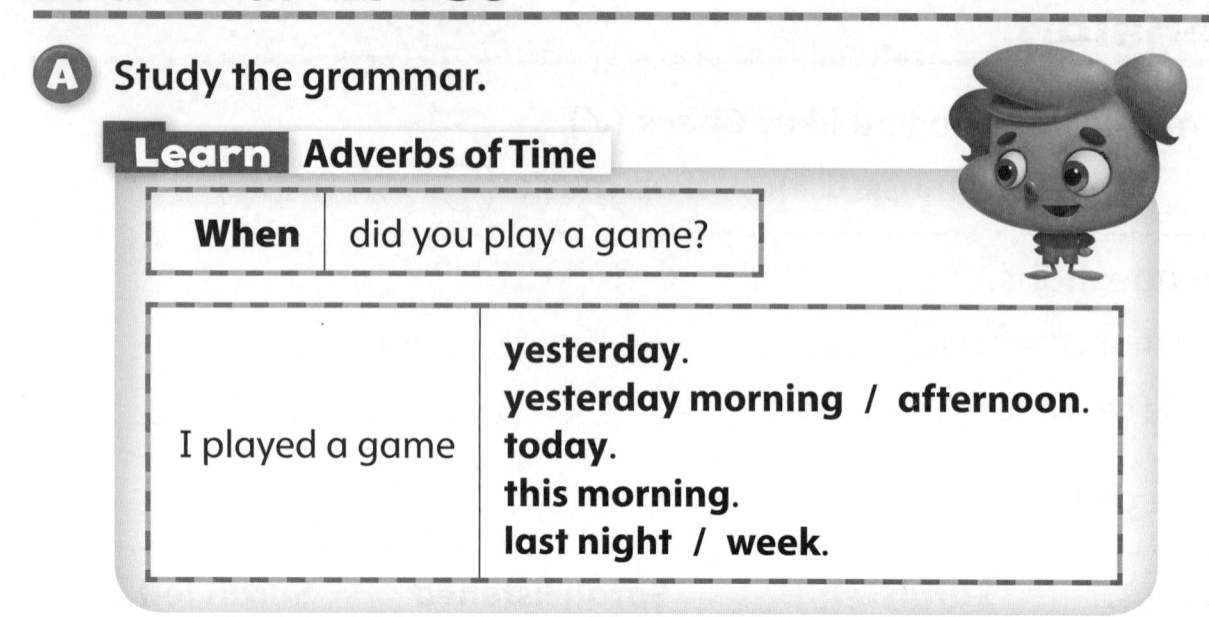

A Study the grammar.

Learn Adverbs of Time

| When | did you play a game? |

| I played a game | yesterday.
yesterday morning / afternoon.
today.
this morning.
last night / week. |

B It's Saturday night. Look at Billy's diary and answer the questions.

last night this morning yesterday morning today ~~yesterday afternoon~~ last week

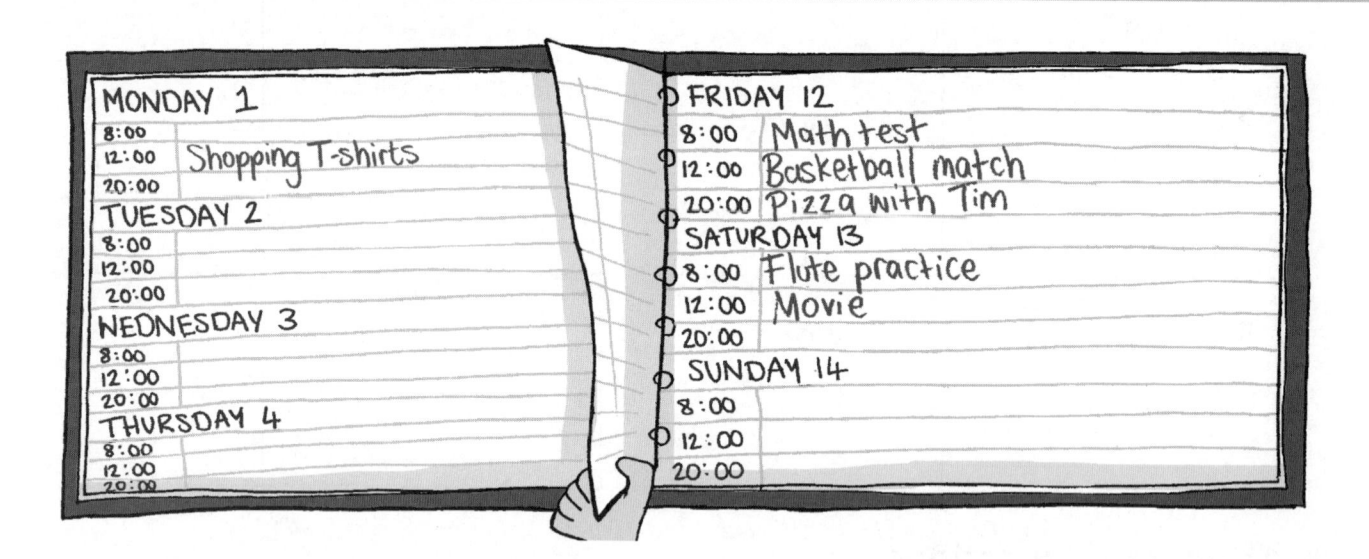

1 When did Billy play basketball?
   yesterday afternoon

2 When did he have a math test?
   _____

3 When did he practice the flute?
   _____

4 When did he go shopping?
   _____

5 When did he see a movie?
   _____

6 When did he have a pizza?
   _____

122 Unit 14 *Grammar: Adverbs of Time*

C Write the questions.

1. yesterday evening / she / practice the drums / did / ?
   Did she practice the drums yesterday evening?
   Yes, she did.

2. you / last night / did / play with your friends / ?
   _____
   No, I didn't.

3. go to the ballet / did / last week / you / ?
   _____
   Yes, we did.

4. did / yesterday / they / bake cookies / ?
   _____
   No, they didn't.

5. go to music class / he / this morning / did / ?
   _____
   Yes, he did.

6. today / did / do subtraction problems / you / ?
   _____
   No, I didn't.

D Answer the questions.

1. When did you have a math test?
   _____

2. When did you play outside?
   _____

3. When did you watch TV?
   _____

4. When did you see your friends?
   _____

Grammar: Adverbs of Time **Unit 14**

Communicate

Words

A Match the beginnings to the ends of the sentences, and the sentences to the pictures.

1. Do — a a concert. — g
2. Sign — b fans. — h
3. Make — c an interview. — i
4. Give — d autographs. — j
5. Have — e a mistake. — k
6. Talk to — f lunch. — l

B Complete the sentences with the simple past of the verbs from **A**.

1. Kelly Taylor _____gave_____ a concert last week.
2. Before the concert she _____ fans.
3. She _____ interview.
4. Before the interview, she _____ lunch.
5. Kelly _____ a mistake at the concert.
6. She _____ autographs after the concert.

124 Unit 2 *Vocabulary: Verb Phrases* Student Book page 142

Writing Study

A Match the beginnings of the sentences to the ends. Write the letters.

1. _e_ Thomas is happy and
2. ___ He can sing, but
3. ___ I like pasta, but
4. ___ You have a trumpet and
5. ___ He talks to fans, but

a I have a flute.
b I don't like salad.
c he doesn't do interviews.
d he can't dance.
e excited.

Writing

A Read about Abdul's favorite music.

> I like piano music. My favorite piano music is fast and sounds like a storm in the rainforest. I like to listen to it in the evening after I do my homework. Sometimes I listen to it with my younger brother.

B Think about your favorite music and what it sounds like. Answer the questions.

1 What music is it? _____
2 What instruments can you hear? _____
3 What do the instruments sound like? _____

_____

4 Do you listen to music with other people? _____

C Now write about your favorite music and what it sounds like.

_____
_____
_____

Writing: Using And *and* But **Unit 14** **125**

What have you learned?

Review

A Complete the chart.

excited smile record proud
wait worried cry unhappy

Feelings	excited
Actions	

B Complete the sentences.

1 We usually h<u>a</u> <u>v</u> <u>e</u> l<u>u</u> <u>n</u> <u>c</u> <u>h</u> in the cafeteria.

2 When you do a math problem wrong, you m__ __ __ a m__ __ __ __ __ __.

3 Musicians play music for a lot of people when they g__ __ __ a c__ __ __ __ __ __.

4 When babies are u__ __ __ __ __ __, they cry.

5 Musicians like to r__ __ __ __ __ __ their music.

BIG QUESTION 7
How does music make us feel?

126

C Look at the chart and write sentences in the correct tense.

	In the Afternoon	Yesterday Afternoon	At Night	Last Night	On Sunday	Last Sunday
Practice the Piano	Jill			Jill	John	
Read Comic Books		Lynne	Andy			Andy
Watch TV			John		Lynne	
Go to the Park	Liz			Liz		John

1 watch TV / on Sunday <u>Lynne watches TV on Sunday.</u>
2 read comic books / yesterday afternoon _____
3 go to the park / in the afternoon _____
4 practice the piano / last night _____
5 watch TV / at night _____
6 practice the piano / in the afternoon _____

D Look at the chart and answer the questions.

1 When did Liz go to the park? <u>Last night.</u>
2 When did Andy read comic books? _____
3 When does Jill practice the piano? _____
4 When does Liz go to the park? _____
5 When does Andy read comic books? _____
6 When did Jill practice the piano? _____

Review 127

BIG QUESTION 8

What makes things move?

Think about the Big Question. Write.

What do you know?

_____
_____
_____
_____
_____
_____

What do you want to know?

_____
_____
_____
_____
_____
_____

UNIT 15 Get Ready

Words

A Circle the odd one out.

1 push   pull   (rescue)
2 movement   feelings   speed
3 easy   hard   sad
4 push   throw   wait
5 light   high   heavy

B Look at the pictures and write the words.

| ground   movement   heavy   ~~push~~ |

1

2

3

4

1. push

C Circle the correct words.
1 When I **(push)** / **pull** something, I am behind it.
2 The book is on the shelf. There **is** / **isn't** movement.
3 Speed is how fast things **move** / **pull**.
4 It's easy to pull a **light** / **heavy** thing.
5 I throw a ball. My friend doesn't catch it. It falls to the **sunlight** / **ground**.
6 I can push and **pull** / **wait** a chair.

D Complete the story.

| easy | push | pushes | movement | heavy | ground | light | ~~pulls~~ |

Johnny and Joey put a lot of snow on their wagon. Joey ___pulls___ (1) the wagon and Johnny _____ (2) it, but it doesn't move. There isn't any _____ (3). The wagon is too _____ (4).

Joey and Johnny have an idea. They _____ (5) a lot of snow off the wagon. The snow falls to the _____ (6). The wagon is _____ (7) now, so it's _____ (8) to pull. The boys are happy.

Vocabulary: Forces   Unit 15   129

Read

A Read the text quickly. Answer the question.

At the end of class, what does Jimmy know a lot about?

Move This!

Jimmy and his class are learning about forces. Ms. Jenkins has two boxes. One is small and has clothes in it; the other is big and has books in it. Ms. Jenkins calls Jimmy to the front.

"Push the small box, Jimmy," says Ms. Jenkins. Jimmy pushes the box.
"It's easy to push," he says.

"Now push the big box, Jimmy," says Ms. Jenkins. Jimmy pushes the box.
"It's hard to push," he says.

"Yes, you're right, Jimmy. The small box is lighter than the big box. We need a small force to move light things, and a big force to move heavy things."

Think
The box is easy to push. The box is light. Which is the cause? Which is the effect?

"Now, Jimmy, push the heavy box with a small force. Good. Now push it with a big force. Which force makes the box move faster, the small force or the big force?"

"The big force. The big force makes the box go further, too."

Think
The box goes fast. Jimmy pushes with a big force. Which is the cause? Which is the effect?

---

130 Unit 15 *Reading: Cause and Effect* Student Book page 149

Understand

Comprehension

A What part of the text do you like? Check (✓).

Jimmy ☐   Ms. Jenkins ☐   Pushing the boxes ☐

B Complete the chart.

Cause	Effect
1 A light thing …	… needs _____ to move it.
2 A _____ thing …	… needs a big force to move it.
3 A _____ force …	… makes the box go fast and far.

C Circle *True* or *False*.

1 Jimmy is in English class.   True   **(False)**
2 Ms. Jenkins is teaching the class about forces.   True   False
3 Ms. Jenkins uses many boxes.   True   False
4 The small box is easy to push.   True   False
5 The big box is easy to push.   True   False

D Read and answer the questions.

Jimmy pushes a light and a heavy box.

1 Which box needs a bigger force to move it? _____
2 Which box is easier to push? _____

Jimmy pushes the heavy box with a small force, then a big force.

3 Which force makes the box go further? _____
4 Which force doesn't make the box go fast? _____

Grammar in Use

A Study the grammar.

Learn Comparatives

fast	fast**er than**
tall	tall**er than**
nice	nic**er than**

heavy	heav**ier than**
easy	eas**ier than**
big	big**ger**

B Write the comparatives.

1 fast _____
2 slow _____
3 small _____
4 big _____
5 light _____
6 heavy _____

C Circle the correct words.

1 An elephant is **smaller** / (**bigger**) than a rabbit.
2 Trains aren't **slower** / **faster** than bicycles.
3 A desk isn't **heavier** / **lighter** than a book.
4 A ruler is usually **shorter** / **longer** than a pencil.

D Write sentences.

1 A cat / not small / a mouse
  A cat isn't smaller than a mouse.
2 Paper / light / wood
  _____
3 A bush / short / a tree
  _____
4 A liquid / not light / a gas
  _____

132   Unit 15   *Grammar: Comparative Adjectives with -er and -ier*   Student Book page 153

E Look at the pictures and write sentences.

1. the white car / big / the black car
   The white car isn't bigger than the black car.

2. a horse / heavy / a goat
   _____

3. the boys / short / the girls
   _____

4. a honeybee / small / a hummingbird
   _____

5. the ruler / long / the pencil case
   _____

6. an airplane / fast / a train
   _____

F Answer the questions.

1. Are you taller than your friend?
   _____

2. Is your pen longer than your pencil?
   _____

3. What is bigger than your backpack?
   _____

4. What is lighter than your book?
   _____

Grammar: Comparative Adjectives with -er and -ier **Unit 15** **133**

Communicate

Words

A Look at the picture and write the words.

> computer mouse   broom   stapler   door   desk drawer   suitcase

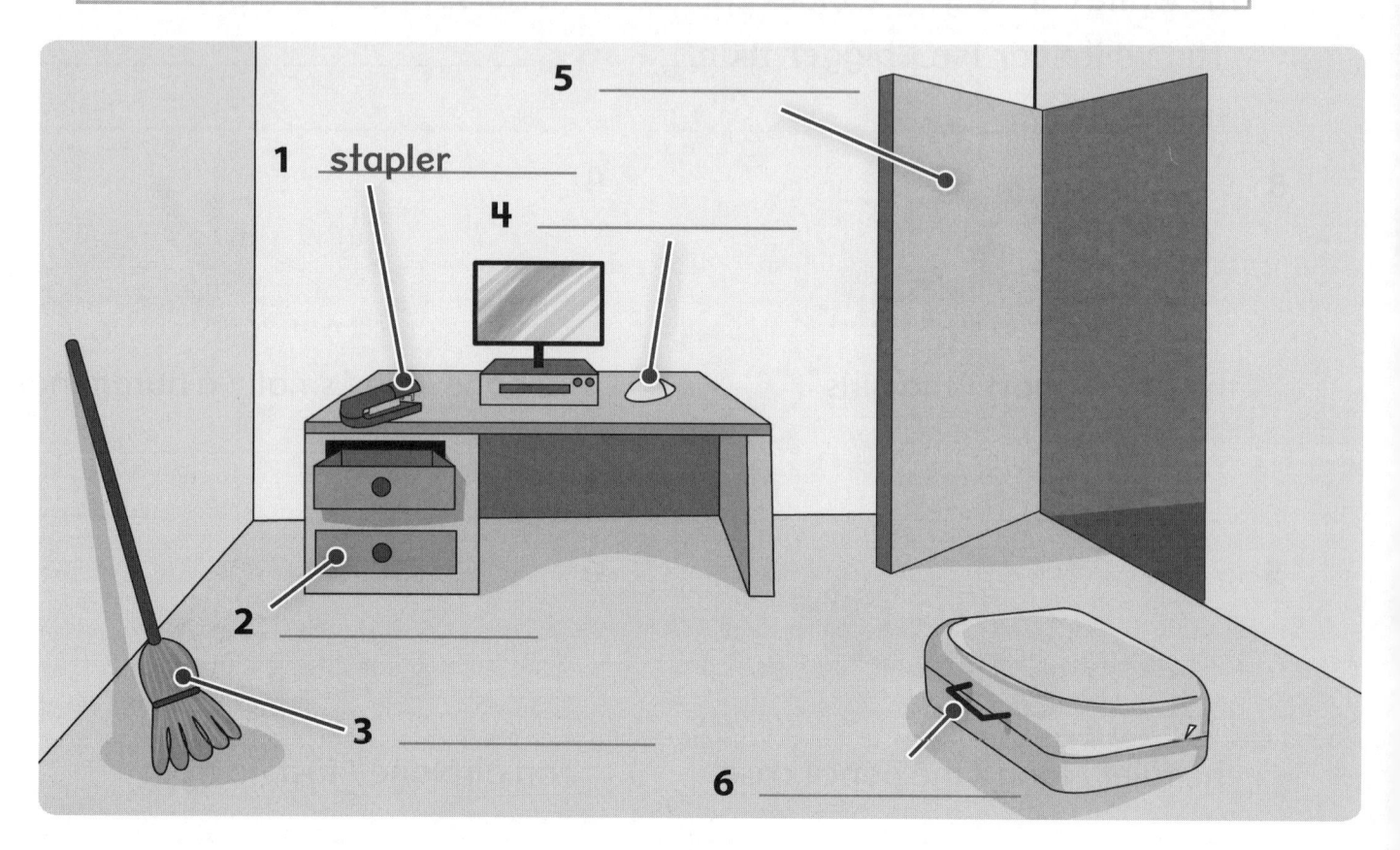

1. stapler
2. _____
3. _____
4. _____
5. _____
6. _____

B Write the words from **A**.

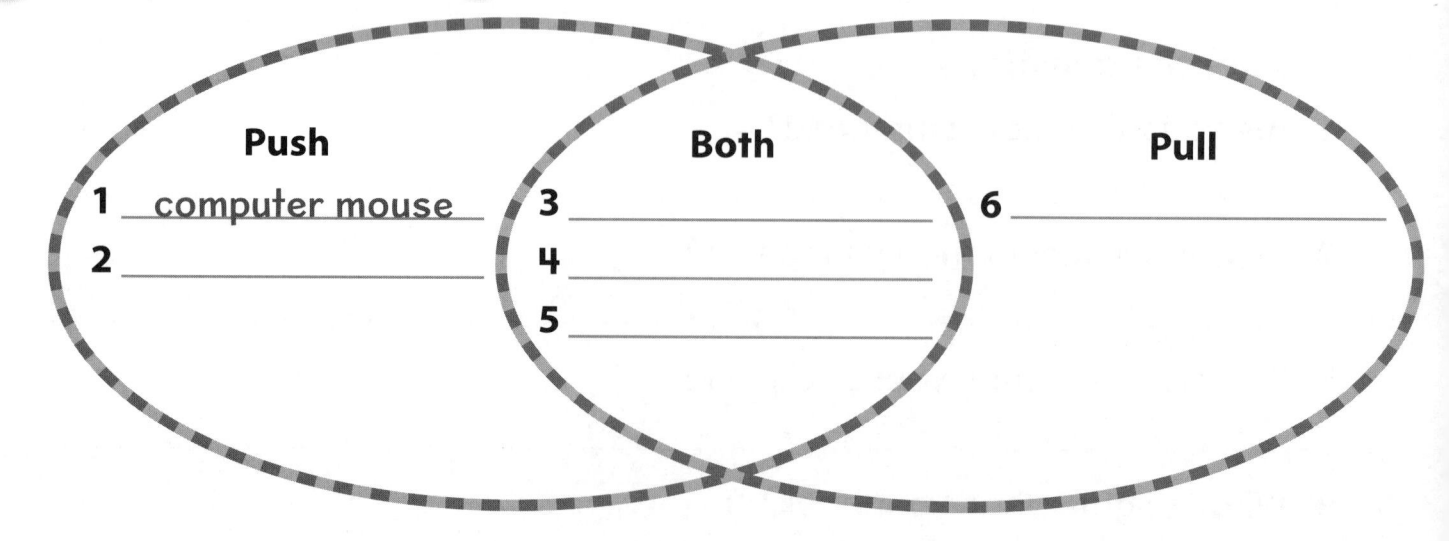

Push
1. computer mouse
2. _____

Both
3. _____
4. _____
5. _____

Pull
6. _____

134   Unit 15   *Communicate: Objects*   Student Book page 154

Word Study

A Match the opposites.

1 fast — d slow
2 dirty — a big
3 small — b cool
4 polite — c plain
5 warm — e rude
6 fancy — f sad
7 loud — g clean
8 happy — h soft

Writing

A Read what Ahmed wrote about something he pushes and something he pulls.

> I push my little sister on the swing at the park. She likes to swing high. I pull the oven door open when I bake cookies with my mother.

B Answer the questions about something you push and something you pull.

1 What do you push? _____
2 Why? _____
3 What do you pull? _____
4 Why? _____

C Now write about those things.

_____
_____
_____

UNIT 16 Get Ready

Words

A Look at the pictures and complete the puzzle.

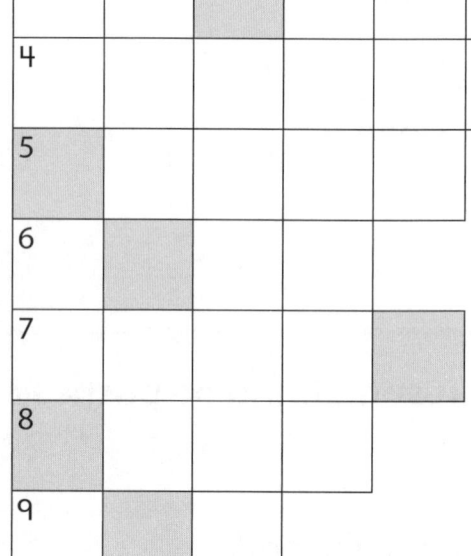

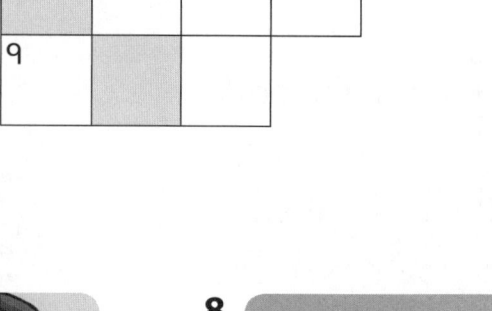

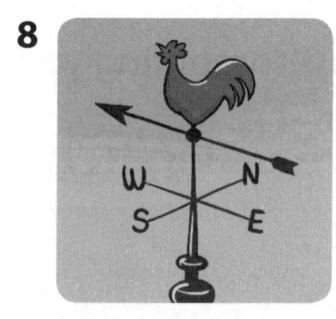

1. forward

B Look at the gray boxes in **A**. Write the letters to make a question. Then answer the question.

H _ _ _ _ _ _ _ _ ?
5 2 8 6 4 9 7 1 3

Unit 16   Vocabulary: Descriptions of Place • Feelings

C Circle the correct answers.

1 A lot of animals live on a _____.
   a shelf   b (mountain)

2 I travel from the _____ to the west.
   a east   b ground

3 When I walk from one place to another place, I move _____.
   a east   b forward

4 It has horns and a cute face. It's a _____.
   a hummingbird   b goat

D Circle the odd one out.

1 mountain   land   (forward)
2 goat   wolf   shelf
3 stubborn   angry   wet
4 horns   gills   mountain
5 goat   lion   fish
6 forward   east   goat

E Complete the sentences.

1 A lot of animals live on that m<u>ountain</u>.
2 He never does the things he doesn't want to do. He's very s_____.
3 When my sister breaks my toy, I feel a_____.
4 After the rain, all the plants were w_____.
5 Careful! That's not a dog, it's a w_____!
6 Goats and other animals have h_____ on their head.
7 There's a lot of traffic, but we are moving f_____.
8 When you travel from the USA to Europe, you go e_____.

Vocabulary: Descriptions of Place • Feelings   Unit 16   137

Read

A Read the story quickly. Answer the question.

What do the boys find in the park?

_____

A Day in the Park

Diego and Julio often play together in the biggest park in town. One day they find an old wagon in the park, and they play with it all day. They push and pull it around the park. Diego pulls Julio, and then Julio pulls Diego. They have fun.

Think
What does the writer want you to know?

It's time to go home. Diego and Julio both want to take the wagon home. They both grab the wagon. "I want the wagon," says Diego. "No! I want the wagon," says Julio. They push and pull the wagon for a long time. It breaks! "I don't want the wagon now," says Diego. "Well, I don't want it now either," says Julio and they leave. They're both angry and unhappy.

Think
What does the writer want you to know?

When they meet two days later, Julio says, "I'm sorry, Diego." "I'm sorry, too," says Diego. "Let's take turns next time." Now both boys know it's not good to be stubborn.

Think
What does the writer want you to know?

138 Unit 16 *Reading: Theme* Student Book page 157

Understand

Comprehension

A What part of the story do you like? Check (✓).

Diego ☐   Julio ☐   The wagon ☐

B Circle the correct theme of the story.

   a Friends should play together often.

   b People shouldn't be stubborn.

   c It's not good to be rude.

C Circle *True* or *False*. For false statements, correct the underlined words. Write the correct words.

1 Diego and Julio live in <u>the country.</u>

   (**True**) **False** _____ a town _____

2 Diego and Julio play in a <u>football pitch.</u>

   True **False** _____

3 Diego and Julio <u>take turns pulling the wagon.</u>

   True **False** _____

4 Diego and Julio fight because they only have <u>one</u> wagon.

   True **False** _____

5 Diego and Julio fight because they are both <u>tall</u>.

   True **False** _____

6 Diego and Julio <u>aren't</u> friends at the end of the story.

   True **False** _____

7 Diego and Julio learn an <u>important</u> lesson that day.

   True **False** _____

Grammar in Use

A Study the grammar

Learn Superlatives

fast	the fast**est**	heavy	the heav**iest**
tall	the tall**est**	easy	the eas**iest**
nice	the nic**est**	big	the bigg**est**

B Write the superlatives.

1 old   _the oldest_
2 slow   _____
3 smart   _____
4 tall   _____

5 heavy   _____
6 big   _____
7 young   _____
8 short   _____

C Circle the correct words.

1 Tom **(is)** / **are** the **(shortest)** / **tallest**.

2 The goats **isn't** / **aren't** the **smallest** / **biggest**.

3 Mary and Annie **is** / **are** the **youngest** / **oldest**.

4 The computer **is** / **are** the **lightest** / **heaviest**.

140 Unit 16 *Grammar: Superlative Adjectives with -est and -iest*

D Look at the picture. Answer the questions.

Jake **Jose** **Abdul**

1 Is Abdul the tallest?
_____

2 Is Jose the shortest?
_____

3 Is Jake's cat the biggest?
_____

4 Is Abdul's cat the biggest?
_____

5 Is Jose's ball the heaviest?
_____

6 Is Jake's ball the lightest?
_____

E Answer the questions.

1 Are you the tallest in your class?
_____

2 Are you the oldest in your family?
_____

3 What's the biggest toy in your room?
_____

4 What's the lightest thing in your backpack?
_____

Grammar: Superlative Adjectives with -est and -iest   Unit 16

Communicate

Words

A Circle the correct words.

1. basketball / (soccer)
2. golf / tennis
3. basketball / hockey
4. baseball / tennis
5. baseball / golf
6. tennis / hockey

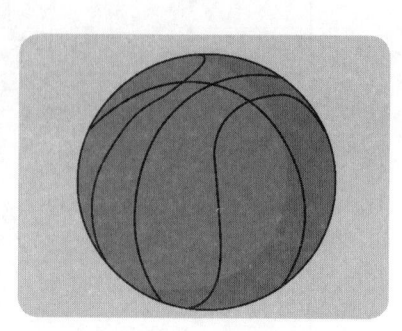

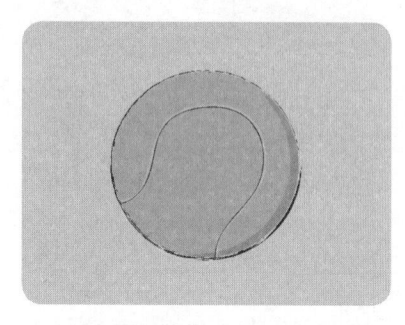

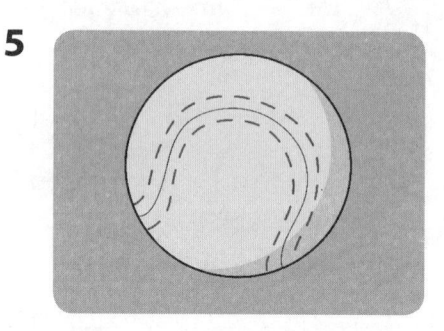

B Write the words from **A**.

1. People play this sport on ice. They need ice skates. _____hockey_____
2. People usually play this game outside in the summer. There's a bat and a ball. _____
3. Two people play this sport. The ball is small and usually yellow. _____
4. Tall people are good at this game. The ball is big and dark orange. _____
5. Two teams play this game. They run and kick the ball. The ball is black and white. _____
6. People play this outside. They hit a very small white ball into a very small hole in the grass. _____

Unit 16   Vocabulary: Sports

Writing Study

A Circle the word that is wrong.

1	**a** small	**b** smaller	**c** the (smalliest)		
2	**a** happy	**b** happier	**c** the happyest		
3	**a** tall	**b** taller	**c** the taller		
4	**a** bigg	**b** bigger	**c** the biggest		
5	**a** heavi	**b** heavier	**c** the heaviest		
6	**a** easy	**b** easyer	**c** the easiest		
7	**a** long	**b** longer	**c** the longer		
8	**a** angry	**b** angrier	**c** the angryest		

Writing

A Read about the speed and movement in the sport Clare likes to play.

> I like hockey. My friends and I always skate fast on the ice. Sometimes we hit the puck with a big force, and sometimes we use a small force. We have fun.

B Think about a sport you like to play. Answer the questions.

1 What sport do you like? _____
2 How do you move? _____
3 Do you move fast? _____
4 Do you use a big or a small force? _____

C Now write about that sport.

_____
_____
_____

What have you learned?

Review

A Look at the pictures and complete the sentences.

1. It's not easy to _____ a _____ suitcase.

2. The _____ pushed each other with their _____.

3. It was raining and the boys were _____ and _____.

4. Maria plays _____ and _____.

5. It's _____ to _____ this door open because it's light.

BIG QUESTION 8
What makes things move?

B Complete the sentences. Use the comparative or superlatives.
1. Henry is ____younger____ than Mike. (young)
2. My father is the _____ in our family. (heavy)
3. Ships are _____ than cars. (big)
4. Are turtles _____ than rabbits? Yes, they are. (slow)
5. Is an eagle the _____ bird on Earth? No, it isn't. (small)
6. What is _____ than a goldfish? A monkey. (smart)

C Match the questions to the answers.
1. Are basketballs bigger than baseballs?   a A couch.
2. Is a chair bigger than a couch?   b Yes, it is.
3. What's heavier than a chair?   c No, they aren't.
4. What's smaller than a basketball?   d Yes, they are.
5. Are chairs longer than couches?   e No, it isn't.
6. Is a basketball heavier than a baseball?   f A baseball.

D Read the answers and complete the questions.
1. ____What is____ faster ____than____ a train?
   An airplane.
2. _____ Billy _____ Johnny?
   Yes, he is. He's the fastest in the school.
3. _____ Kevin _____ boy in the class?
   No, he isn't. He's the shortest.
4. _____ smaller _____ a hummingbird?
   A honeybee.
5. _____ you _____ person in your family?
   No, I'm not. My sister is younger than me.

Review 145

BIG QUESTION 9

How do we make art?

Think about the Big Question. Write.

What do you know?

_____
_____
_____
_____
_____
_____

What do you want to know?

_____
_____
_____
_____
_____
_____

UNIT 17 Get Ready

Words

A Look at the instructions. Color the picture.

Stars are green.	Ovals are orange.
Crescents are pink.	Spirals are blue.

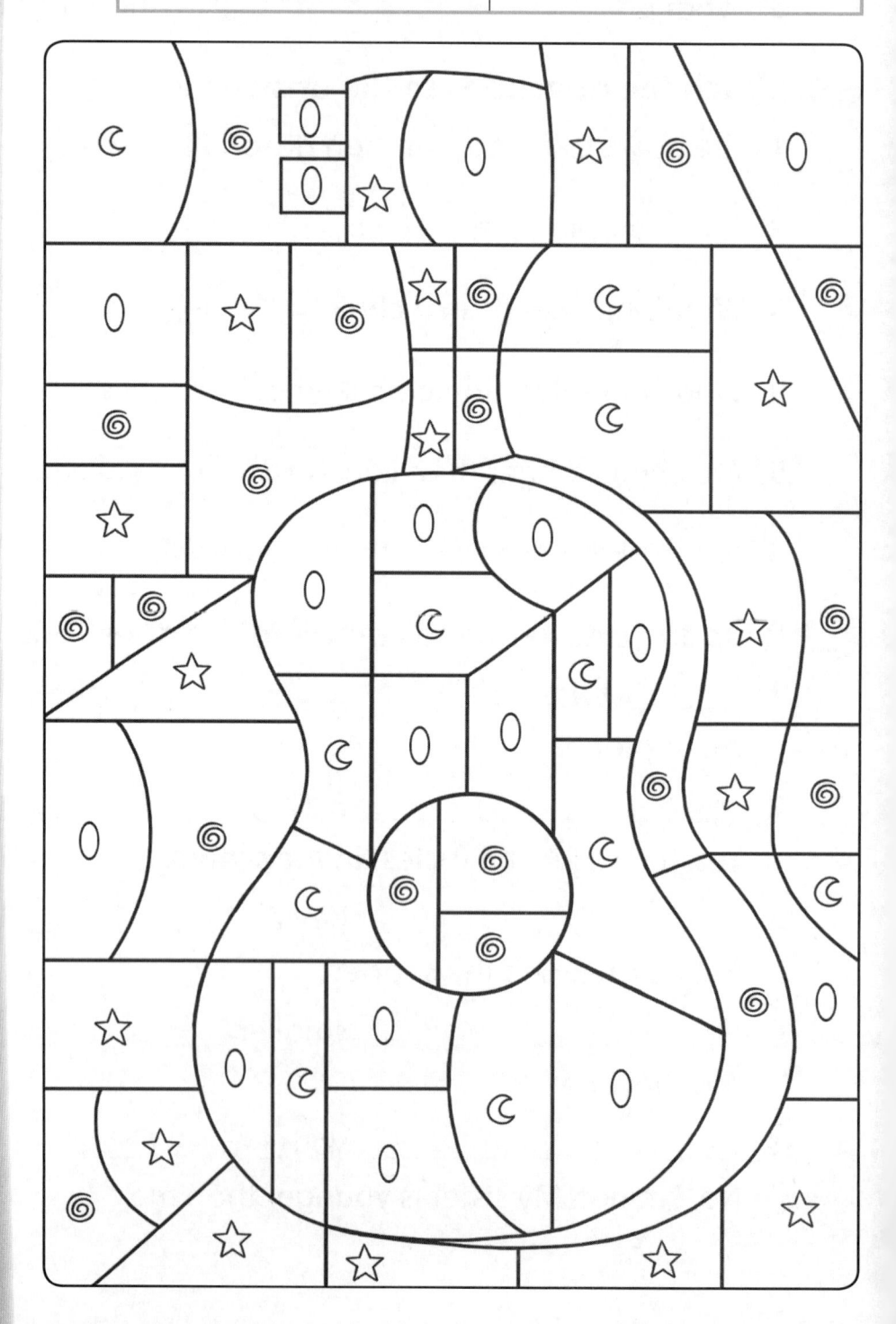

Unit 17 · Vocabulary: Art • Shapes · Student Book page 168

B Write the words.

collage	corner	nature	straight	~~pattern~~	circle

1  pattern

2   _____

3 _____

4 _____

5 _____

6 _____

C Circle *True* or *False*.

1 An egg is an oval. — (**True**) **False**

2 A circle is a straight line. — **True** **False**

3 A star is round. — **True** **False**

4 All sculptures are big and made of wood. — **True** **False**

5 Nature has living and nonliving things in it. — **True** **False**

6 A collage is made of one picture. — **True** **False**

Read

A Read the text quickly. Answer the question.

How does the boy draw the dinosaur?

Drawing a Dinosaur

It's fun to draw things with shapes. Read the text and draw a dinosaur using shapes.

Think

Think about things at home that are ovals and circles.

Let's start.

Draw a small oval for the head, then draw a big oval for the body. Draw two straight lines from the head to the body. Draw three triangles on top of the small oval. Draw two small circles inside the head for the eyes. Then draw two very small circles next to each other under the eyes. This is the nose.

Draw a few small triangles on top of the body. Color all the triangles black. Draw half a crescent in the middle of the big circle for the tail. Leave one end of the crescent open. Draw two rectangles under the body, one on the right side and one on the left side. Now color your dinosaur, and give it a name.

Think

Think about the things you can draw using shapes.

148 Unit 17 Reading: Text-to-Self Connection

Student Book page 169

Understand

Comprehension

A What part of the text do you like? Check (✓).

The instructions ☐   Using shapes ☐   The picture ☐

B Answer the questions.

1. How many different shapes are there in the drawing?
   <u>There are five shapes.</u>

2. What shape is the head?
   _____

3. What shape is the body?
   _____

4. What shape do you draw for the eyes?
   _____

5. What shape do you draw for the legs?
   _____

6. How many triangles do you draw?
   _____

7. How many circles do you draw?
   _____

8. Do we always use shapes in drawings?
   _____

C Draw something with shapes. Then write how to draw it.

Step 1 _____
_____
_____

Step 2 _____
_____
_____

Step 3 _____
_____
_____

Step 4 _____
_____
_____

What is it? _____

Grammar in Use

A Study the grammar.

Learn Quantifiers

	some	
There is / I have	a little	paper.
	a lot of	
	some	
There are / I have	a few	pens.
	a lot of	

There isn't / I don't have	any	paper.
There aren't / I don't have		pens.

B Circle the correct words.

1 The teacher doesn't have **some** / **(any)** paint.

2 There were **a little** / **a few** circles in the picture.

3 There isn't **a few** / **any** art in the library.

4 I have **a few** / **any** notebooks in my backpack.

5 There are **any** / **some** stars in the sky.

6 My mother puts **a little** / **a lot of** carrots in the soup.

C Complete the sentences.

1 Nancy has _____ oranges.
(many / some)

2 Kai has _____ chips.
(a few / a lot of)

3 Debbie has _____ sandwiches.
(a lot of / some)

4 Jack doesn't have _____ cookies.
(any / a few)

D Look at the picture and complete the sentences.

1. There is ____a lot of____ red paint.
2. There aren't _____ pens.
3. There is _____ yellow paint.
4. There is _____ blue paint.
5. There isn't _____ green paint.

E Rewrite each sentence.

1. There is some salad on the table. (vegetables)
   There are some vegetables on the table.
2. They have a lot of paper. (any)
   _____
3. There aren't any crayons in the classroom. (some)
   _____
4. We have a few cookies. (paint)
   _____

F Complete the sentences.

1. I have a few _____ in my room.
2. I have some _____ in my room.
3. I have a lot of _____ in my room.
4. I don't have any _____ in my room.
5. There isn't any _____ in my room.
6. There aren't any _____ in my room.

Grammar: Quantifiers with Count and Non Count Nouns **Unit 17** **151**

Communicate

Words

A Match the words to the pictures.

1. mobile
2. oil painting
3. origami
4. photograph
5. drawing
6. mosaic

a. 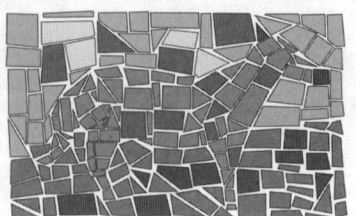
b. 
c. 
d. 
e. 
f.

B Look at the pictures. Write the words.

1. __photograph__
2. _____ 
3. _____

152   Unit 17   Vocabulary: Art   Student Book page 174

Word Study

A Circle the word that is wrong. Write the correct word.

1 He bought (ate) comic books. _____eight_____

2 This is there house. _____

3 That subtraction problem isn't write. _____

4 Can you sea the ovals in the painting? _____

5 There are too stars in the mosaic. _____

6 Eye used spirals and crescents in my collage. _____

Writing

A Read about the shapes Brian uses in art.

> I love drawing. I use squares and rectangles for the house, windows and doors. I use circles and ovals for the flowers and the sun. I use triangles for the trees. My drawing looks great!

B Think about your favorite kind of art and the shapes you use in art. Answer the questions.

1 What is your piece of art? _____

2 What shapes do you use? What are they for?
_____
_____
_____

3 How does your art look? _____

C Now write about using shapes in your art.
_____
_____
_____

UNIT 18 Get Ready

Words

A Look at the pictures and write the words.

~~shiny~~ climb crumple waves fold crane golden edge seal

1. shiny
2. 
3. 
4. 
5. 
6. 
7. 
8. 
9.

154　Unit 18　*Vocabulary: Art*　　　　Student Book page 176

B Look at the pictures and complete the puzzle. Then write the mystery word.

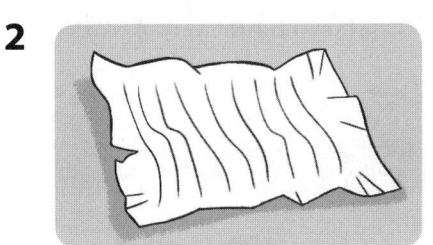

1 2 3
4 5 6

			s	h	i	n	y
2							
		3					
			4				
			5				
	6						

The mystery word is: s_____

C Match the beginnings of the sentences to the ends.

1 The sun is sometimes   a we need to fold it.
2 It is dangerous to stand on   b like to climb trees.
3 To make a piece of paper into a bird   c a beautiful golden color.
4 Many boys and girls   d seals swimming in the ocean.
5 We can sometimes see   e the edge of a desk.

Vocabulary: Art Unit 18 **155**

Read

A Read the story quickly. Answer the question.

What does Kai use for the ground in the picture?

A Mother's Day Present

Kai likes art. He wants to make a special picture for his mother for Mother's Day. He does a drawing of his mother outside in the sun. He wants to make his picture interesting, but he doesn't know how.

Think
Think about a difficult picture you wanted to make.

He asks his art teacher for help.

Think
Think about the people you asked for help.

She gives him some good ideas. She tells him to crumple dark blue paper and put it at the top for the sky.

Kai thinks, "I can use yellow paper for the sun and small stones in different colors for mountains."

Think
Think about the help they gave you.

He uses glue to stick the stones to the paper. He uses a little sand for his mother and some pasta for the ground. He finishes the picture and takes it home.

Think
Were you happy about the picture in the end?

He gives his mother the collage for Mother's Day. She loves it and puts it on the wall.

Understand

Comprehension

A What part of the story do you like? Check (✓).

Kai ☐   The teacher ☐   The collage ☐

B Answer the questions.
1. What school subject does Kai like? _____
2. Who does Kai ask for help? _____
3. Why does he ask for help? _____
4. Does Kai use pasta and sand in his collage? _____

C Circle *True* or *False*.

1 Kai loves his mother very much.	(True)	False
2 In the beginning Kai's picture has colors in it.	True	False
3 Kai draws a picture of his mother in the sunlight.	True	False
4 Kai's art teacher has good ideas.	True	False
5 Kai makes a paper collage.	True	False
6 Kai uses different yellow things.	True	False
7 Kai is unhappy with his picture.	True	False
8 Kai's family can see his picture every day.	True	False

D Think of something special you made for someone. Answer the questions.
1. What did you make? _____
2. Who did you make it for? _____
3. What did you use? _____
4. How did you make it? _____
5. Did the person like it? _____

Grammar in Use

A Study the grammar.

Learn Quantifiers

Was there	any	paper?
Were there		crayons?

How	much	paper	**was** there?
	many	crayons	**were** there?

There	was	some / a little / a lot of	paper.
	were	some / a few / a lot of / ten	crayons.

B Circle the correct words. Then match the questions to the answers.

1 Was / (Were) there any pencils? •   • a No, there wasn't.

2 How **much** / **many** trash was there? •   • b Yes, there were.

3 How **much** / **many** fruit did she buy? • • c He ate three cookies.

4 **Were** / **Was** there any paint in the jar? • • d She bought a lot of fruit.

5 How **much** / **many** cookies did he eat? • • e There were a few children.

6 How **much** / **many** goats were on the mountain? • • f There was a little trash.

7 Were there **much** / **many** children? • • g There were five goats.

C Look at the pictures. Answer the questions.

1 Did he have any paint?
   No, he didn't.

2 How many stars did she make?
   _____

3 How many cranes were there?
   _____

4 Was there any paper?
   _____

5 How much snow was there?
   _____

6 Did she draw any shapes?
   _____

D Answer the questions.

1 Did you have any milk today?
_____

2 Did you see any cranes yesterday?
_____

3 How much paper is there in your bedroom?
_____

4 How many pens and pencils are there in your backpack?
_____

Grammar: Questions with Quantifiers **Unit 18**

Communicate

Words

A Find and circle the words.

1 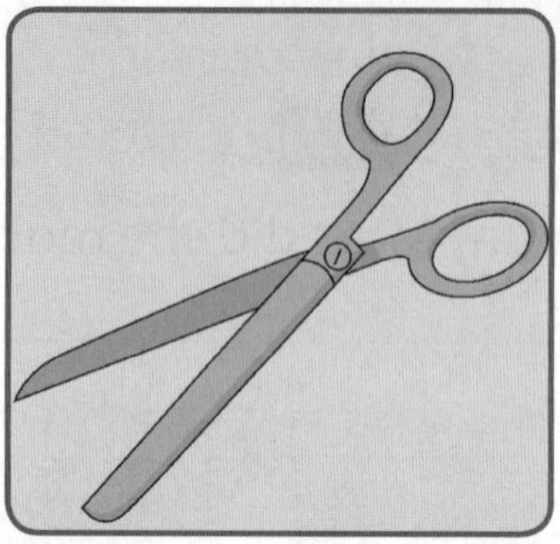
2 
3 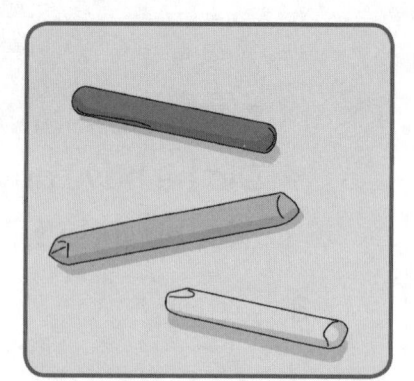
4 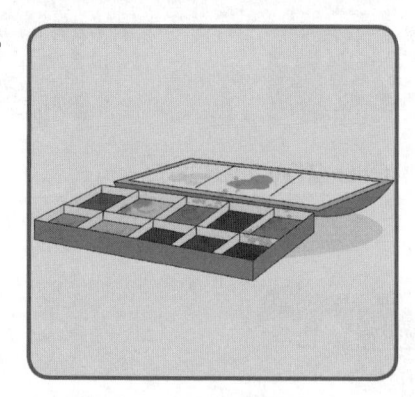
5 
6

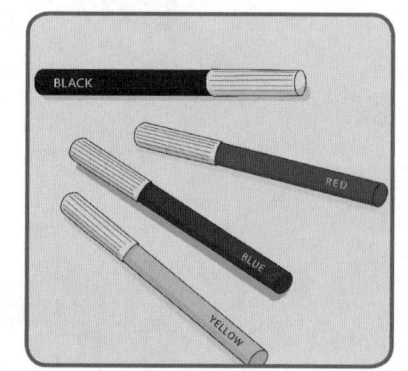

x	t	n	w	a	t	e	r	c	o	l	o	r	s	u	i
m	a	r	k	e	r	s	a	t	z	c	h	a	l	k	m
b	g	l	u	e	f	p	s	c	i	s	s	o	r	s	q
c	o	l	o	r	e	d	p	e	n	c	i	l	s	g	k

B Complete the chart with words from **A**.

Things We Use To Color A Picture	Things We Don't Use To Color A Picture
1 _____watercolors_____	5 _____
2 _____	6 _____
3 _____	
4 _____	

160   Unit 18   *Vocabulary: Art Tools*   Student Book page 182

Writing Study

A Are the commas correct? Write (✓) or (✗). Rewrite the incorrect sentences.

1 Hank used colored pencils scissors, and glue for his collage. _X_
   Hank used colored pencils, scissors, and glue for his collage.

2 They ran, jumped, and played on the playground. ___
   _____

3 My dog is smart gentle and patient. ___
   _____

4 We saw oil paintings, mosaics and photographs at the museum. ___
   _____

Writing

A Read about the tools Emily uses in her art projects.

> I usually use colored pencils in my drawings. I use markers for posters. I use scissors and glue when I make a collage. I hardly ever use chalk or watercolors.

B Think about the tools you use for your art projects, and complete the chart.

I usually use …	I hardly ever use …
_____ for _____	_____
_____ for _____	_____

C Now write about the tools you use for your art projects.

_____
_____
_____
_____

Writing: Using Commas in Lists **Unit 18**

What have you learned?

Review

A Complete the chart.

~~watercolors~~ origami star sculpture oval glue chalk collage markers scissors mobile crescent spiral photograph mosaic

Art Supplies	1	watercolors
	2	
	3	
	4	
	5	
Art Projects	6	
	7	
	8	
	9	
	10	
	11	
Shapes	12	
	13	
	14	
	15	

BIG QUESTION 9

How do we make art?

B Circle the correct words.

1 John has **(some)** / **any** colored pencils.
2 There is **a few** / **a little** glue on the table.
3 Were there **any** / **some** circles in the sculpture?
4 How **many** / **much** markers do you need?
5 There are **any** / **a lot of** oil paintings in the museum.
6 How **many** / **much** chalk is there?

C Look at the pictures. Answer the questions.

1 Did he have any chalk?
   No, he didn't.

2 How many origami animals did she make?
   _____

3 Were there many markers on the desk?
   _____

4 How much paint did he use?
   _____

5 Was there any paper on the desk?
   _____

Student's Writing Resource

Writing Process

BEFORE YOU WRITE:
- Read the example text.
- Think about what it means.
- Think about your own ideas.
- Choose an idea to write about.

WHEN YOU WRITE:
- Start your sentences with a capital letter.
- Use punctuation: commas, periods, and question marks.
- Write full sentences.
- Think about your spelling. Look in the dictionary if you don't know.

AFTER YOU WRITE:
- Read your text.
- Correct your mistakes.
- Ask your friend or teacher to read your text.

M
~~m~~y name is George.

My favorite animal group is ~~amphibeans~~. *amphibians*

I like frogs.

They have wet skin, gills, and big eyes.

What is your favorite animal group?

Checklist

I can check my work for:
- punctuation ✓
- spelling ✓
- full sentences ✓

I can correct my mistakes. ✓

164 Student's Writing Resource

Capital Letters

ABC Capital Letters for Names

The first letter of a name is a capital letter.

Billy **G**us **L**ayla **D**ot

ABC Capital Letters in Sentences

The first letter of a sentence is a capital letter.

The liquid is very hot.

I like mammals the best.

My triangles are green.

Punctuation

, Commas

Commas separate three or more words in a list.

I like oranges, apples, and plums.

She was proud, happy, and excited.

My friends come from Italy, Egypt, Sweden, and Australia.

' Apostrophes and contractions

Use an apostrophe when you make a contraction.

She is not seven.   She isn't seven.

They were not tired.   They weren't tired.

Amelia does not like coffee.   Amelia doesn't like coffee.

He did not go to the park.   He didn't go to the park.

You should not eat a lot of candy.   You shouldn't eat a lot of candy.

Jose cannot do his homework.   Jose can't do his homework.

Frogs do not have feathers.   Frogs don't have feathers.

Parts of Speech

Nouns

Nouns are naming words. A noun is a person, place, or thing.

This is my **brother**.

I live in **Mexico**.

Where are your **toys**?

Verbs

Verbs are action words. They show the time of an action.

We **go** to school by bus. (usually happens)

We're **going** to school by bus. (happening now)

We **went** to school by bus. (happened in the past)

Adjectives

Adjectives describe nouns. They tell you more about the nouns.

The statue is **big** and **old**.

It's a **windy** day.

Harry feels **unhappy** and **lonely**.

Subject-Verb Agreement

When you're writing, check that you have the correct form of the verb.

He was in the kitchen this morning.

They are very excited about the party.

We weren't hungry at lunchtime.

Regular and Irregular Verbs

Regular Verbs

Most verbs are regular. Add -ed to form the past tense of regular verbs.

He camp**ed** in the forest.

He fish**ed** in the lake.

He surf**ed** in the sea.

Irregular Verbs

Some verbs are irregular. We don't use -ed to form the past tense. We have to learn the past tense form of each verb. Below is a list of irregular verbs.

Base Verb	Past Simple
beat	beat
bite	bit
blow	blew
buy	bought
catch	caught
choose	chose
cry	cried
do	did
drink	drank
eat	ate
fall	fell
fly	flew
get	got
give	gave

Base Verb	Past Simple
grow	grew
have	had
make	made
put	put
run	ran
sell	sold
shake	shook
sing	sang
sleep	slept
swim	swam
take	took
teach	taught
think	thought
throw	threw

Student's Writing Resource

OXFORD
UNIVERSITY PRESS

Great Clarendon Street, Oxford, OX2 6DP, United Kingdom

Oxford University Press is a department of the University of Oxford.
It furthers the University's objective of excellence in research, scholarship,
and education by publishing worldwide. Oxford is a registered trade
mark of Oxford University Press in the UK and in certain other countries

© Oxford University Press 2014

The moral rights of the author have been asserted

First published in 2014

2018 2017 2016 2015 2014
10 9 8 7 6 5 4 3 2 1

No unauthorized photocopying

All rights reserved. No part of this publication may be reproduced, stored
in a retrieval system, or transmitted, in any form or by any means, without
the prior permission in writing of Oxford University Press, or as expressly
permitted by law, by licence or under terms agreed with the appropriate
reprographics rights organization. Enquiries concerning reproduction outside
the scope of the above should be sent to the ELT Rights Department, Oxford
University Press, at the address above

You must not circulate this work in any other form and you must impose
this same condition on any acquirer

Links to third party websites are provided by Oxford in good faith and for
information only. Oxford disclaims any responsibility for the materials
contained in any third party website referenced in this work

ISBN: 978 0 19 427866 9

Printed in China

This book is printed on paper from certified and well-managed sources

ACKNOWLEDGEMENTS

Illustrated characters Billy, Dot, Gus and Layla by: Luispa Salmon/Lemonade Illustration Agency

Illustrations by: Peter Bay Alexandersen/Shannon Associates L.L.C pp.12, 30, 58, 66, 84, 94, 102, 109, 120, 130, 138, 148, 156; Kathy Baxendale p.39; Clare Elsom/NB Illustration pp.6 (Ex B), 14 (Ex B), 25, 33, 42 (Ex B), 51, 60 (Ex C), 69, 79, 87, 96 (Ex B), 97, 105, 115, 122 (Ex B), 133, 140 (Ex C), 141, 150 (Ex C), 151, 159; Lisa Hunt/The Organisation pp.8, 16 (Ex B), 17, 18, 26, 27, 34, 35, 36, 44, 45, 52, 55, 62, 63, 70, 71, 72, 73, 80, 81, 88, 89, 90, 91, 98, 99, 107, 108, 116, 117, 124, 125, 127, 134, 135, 142, 143, 144, 152, 153, 160, 161, 163; Genevieve Kote pp.2, 10, 11, 20, 21, 28, 29, 38, 46, 56, 64, 74, 82, 83, 92, 100, 101, 110, 111, 118, 128, 129, 136, 146, 154, 155.

The Publishers would like to thank the following for their kind permission to reproduce photographs and other copyright material: Alamy pp.3 (frog/Scott Camazine), 3 (bird/F1online digitale Bildagentur GmbH), 3 (fish scales/imagebroker), 4 (lion/Anna Hair), 16 (ant/Nigel Cattlin), 16 (lynx/Juniors Bildarchiv GmbH), 16 (spider/Paul Springett A), 16 (lion/Image Source), 22 (JTB MEDIA CREATION, Inc.), 39 (radio/Chuck Eckert), 39 (airplane/John Zada), 40 (antique airplane/GL Archive), 47 (Peter Titmuss), 48 (immigration/Niday Picture Library), 48 (woman writing/ClassicStock), 112 (Andres Rodriguez), 147 (collage/amana images inc.); Ardea p.4 (whale/M. Watson); Getty Images pp.3 (feather/Tokism), 16 (chimpanzee/Cyril Ruoso/JH Editorial), 40 (new airplane/2006 AFP), 76 (Rayman), 147 (field/ingmar wesemann); Oxford University Press pp.3 (eggs/Robert Read), 3 (fish/Stockbyte), 147 (ruler/Photodisc); shutterstock pp.16 (lion/Volodymyr Goinyk), 39 (child/Stanislav Komogorov), 39 (globe/beboy), 147 (pattern/Pitball23); Zooid Pictures p.39 (letter)

Cover illustration: Michael Slack

Cover photograph: Craig van der Lende/Getty Images